FOOTBALL

BY JOHN F. GRABOWSKI

Lucent Books, Inc.
San Diego, California

Titles in The History of Sports series include:
Baseball
Basketball
Football
Golf
Hockey
Soccer

Library of Congress Cataloging-in-Publication Data

Grabowski, John F.
    Football / by John F. Grabowski.
        p.   cm. — (History of sports)
    Includes bibliographical references (p.   ) and index.
    ISBN 1-56006-743-8
    1. Football—United States—History—Juvenile literature.
  [1. Football—History.] I. Title. II. Series.
  GV950.7. .G73   2001
  796.332'0973—dc21   00-010086

Copyright © 2001 by Lucent Books, Inc.
P.O. Box 289011, San Diego, CA 92198-9011
Printed in the U.S.A.

Contents

FOREWORD

MORE THAN MANY areas of human endeavor, sports give us the opportunity to see the possibilities in our physical selves. As participants, we all too quickly find limits to how fast we can run, how high we can jump, how far and straight we can hit a golf ball. But as spectators we can surpass those limits as we view the accomplishments of others and see how fast, how smooth, and how strong a human being can be. We marvel at the gravity-defying leaps of a Michael Jordan as he strains towards a basketball hoop or at the dribbling of a Mia Hamm as she eludes defenders on the soccer field. We shake our heads in disbelief at the talents of a young Tiger Woods hitting an approach shot to the green or the speed of a Carl Lewis as he appears to glide around an Olympic track.

These are what the sports media call "the oohs and ahhs" of sports—the stuff of highlight reels and *Sports Illustrated* covers. But to understand a sport only in the context of its most artistic modern athletes is shortsighted, for it does little justice to the accomplishments of the athletes *or* to the sport itself. Far more wise is to view a sport as a continuum—a constantly moving, evolving process. On this continuum are not only the superstars of today, but the people who first played the sport, who thought about rules and strategies that would make it more challenging to play as well as a delight to watch.

Lucent Books' series, *The History of Sports,* provides such a continuum. Each book explores the development of a sport from its basic roots onward, and tries to answer questions that a reader might wonder about. Who were its first players, and what sorts of rules did the sport have then? What kinds of equipment were used in the beginning and what changes have taken place over the years?

Each title in *The History of Sports* also identifies key individuals in the sport's history—people whose leadership or skills have made a difference in the way the sport is played today. Included will be the easily recognized names, the Mia Hamms and the Sammy Sosas, the Wilt Chamberlains and the Wilma Rudolphs. But there are also the names of past greats, people like baseball's King Kelly, soccer's Sir Stanley Matthews, and basketball's Hank Luisetti—who may be less familiar today, but were as synonymous with their sports at one time as the "oohs and ahhs" players of today.

Finally, the series looks at the aspects of a sport that are particularly important in its current point on the continuum. Baseball today is better understood knowing about salary caps and union negotiators. One cannot truly know modern soccer without knowing about the specter of fan violence at matches. And learning about the role of instant replay is critical to a thorough understanding of today's professional football games. In viewing a sport as a continuum, the strides that have been made along the way are that much more admirable. It is a richer view, and one that shows how yesterday's limits have been surpassed—and how the limits of today are the possibilities of athletes in the future.

A Collision Sport

FROM ITS EARLIEST beginnings, football has been a favorite sport at colleges around the country. The professional game, however, was slow to catch on. For the first half of the twentieth century, major league baseball was far and away the most popular spectator sport, winning the title of "America's national pastime."

In 1961, a Gallup Poll sports survey showed that 34 percent of adults questioned said baseball was their favorite sport, while 21 percent opted for football. Eleven years later, the results were quite different. In 1972, 36 percent named football as their favorite, only 21 percent cited baseball.

Why has football made such great strides in becoming the number one sport in the hearts of American adults? The answer likely lies with television.

Football is the ideal television sport. With twenty-two men scrambling about on every play, there are many things happening on a football field that go unnoticed by a spectator. Linemen from both teams attack each other in a battle of three-hundred-pound hulks. Receivers run pass routes all over the field and runners pick their way through openings, all attempting to avoid pursuers intent on bringing them down to earth as violently as possible. With so much going on at the same time, it is impossible to see every action and reaction.

Television, however, makes it possible. Each burst of game activity is followed by a break in the action. During this pause, instant

Fans of the St. Louis Rams react to an exciting play as they watch the telecast of Super Bowl XXXIV.

replay and slow motion allow viewers to see the previous play from every angle imaginable, catching things that fans, coaches, players, and officials would otherwise miss. Color commentators analyze every nuance and subtlety, allowing the viewer to enter a world with a language all its own. As broadcaster—and former player—Pat Summerall once observed, "It's almost as if when the game was invented, it was invented for television. . . . The field is like a stage on which you can see all twenty-two actors, plus the supporting cast on the sidelines. Then the action comes to a stop, and the team goes back into the huddle, which gives you a chance to talk with your buddy and think about what might happen next."[1]

Baseball has no need for such close analysis. Because there are thirteen players, at most, on the field at any one time (nine men on defense, three men on base, and one batter), a fan who follows the path of the ball usually has little trouble tracking any important action. This is also the case in basketball and hockey, where even fewer participants perform on a much smaller playing field. Television does enhance each of these pastimes, but not to the same degree as on the gridiron.

Another factor adding to the game's appeal is the schedule. With one game a week per team the usual allotment, the buildup and anticipation that develop over the intervening six days make the contest more of an event than other major team sports. No one ever complains that the football season is too long, as many do about baseball, basketball, and hockey. "The infrequency of play," explains Baltimore Ravens owner, Art Modell, "makes

each Sunday something special, whether you're in front of your TV set or at the stadium."[2] Nowhere is the excitement more evident than in the period leading up to the Super Bowl, which has become a media event in and of itself.

The time between plays—and between games—gives the fan plenty of time to employ something as American as the hot dog: the second guess. There is ample opportunity to demonstrate one's knowledge of the game and to explain why the fan's play was a better choice than the one picked by the coach. The fan is never wrong, at least from his or her perspective at home in front of the television screen.

Football has often been called a contact sport, but legendary Green Bay Packers

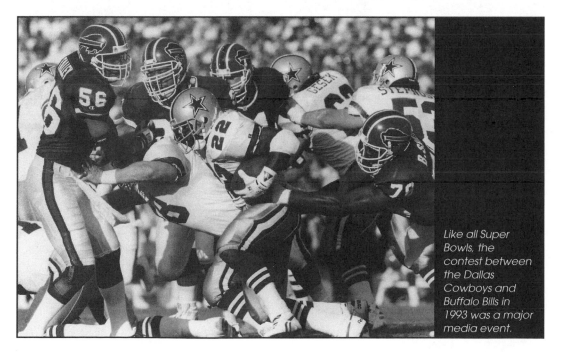

Like all Super Bowls, the contest between the Dallas Cowboys and Buffalo Bills in 1993 was a major media event.

coach Vince Lombardi scoffed at that description. "Dancing is a contact sport," said Lombardi. "Football is a collision sport."[3] The physical component of the game cannot be minimized as an explanation for its popularity. Touch football may be fun to play in the streets, but would not draw millions of viewers on television. The quarterback who leads his team to the winning touchdown in the final seconds of a game may get all the headlines, but the linebacker who makes a key sack or stops a run with a bone-crushing tackle is just as admired.

To many players, the physical contact is the most appealing part of the game. Most would agree with former Baltimore linebacker Mike Curtis who said, "I play football because it's the only place you can hit people and get away with it."[4] The same mind-set applies to offensive players as well. Former Green Bay fullback Jim Taylor was a perfect example. "Jimmy Taylor . . . was a physical animal," remarked former 49er Charlie Krueger. "He preferred running right over you instead of around you. . . . He loved that contact."[5] To fans, the physical element is what separates their sport from all the rest. It is the key ingredient that has made football the favorite pastime of millions of fans across the nation.

CHAPTER 1

The Evolution of Rugby Football

GAMES INVOLVING KICKING an object toward some sort of target have been around for more than two millennia. Whether the object is a leather ball filled with sawdust, an inflated bladder of a slaughtered animal, or the skull of an enemy slain in battle, the satisfaction found in kicking it with the feet cannot be denied.

The Egyptians played a game similar to soccer that had to do with their fertility rites. "Harpaston," in which two teams tried to kick, pass, or carry a ball over the other team's goal line, was played by the ancient Greeks. Roman forces eventually spread their own version of the game, known as "calcio," throughout Europe, all the way to Great Britain. Each of these pastimes, however, had little in common with our modern game of football. Its forebears would come much later.

The Birth of Rugby

During the Middle Ages, contests known as "mellays" developed in Britain. Two teams, each of which might consist of dozens of players, pushed and shoved each other in an effort to move an inflated ball across the opposition's goal line. The game became a tradition among British schoolboys, who played it annually on Shrove Tuesday before Lent. Although the roughness of the game gave rise to attempts at banning it, the soccer-style pastime survived for many years.

It was during one such game at the Rugby School in 1823 that a most unusual event took place. Game time ended at five o'clock in the afternoon. As a matter of custom, when the bell in the nearby tower began to chime, the ball would be placed on the ground and a free kick taken. On this day, however, a schoolboy named William Webb Ellis decided to take matters into his own hands—literally. He set the ball down and tried to kick it, but missed. Frustrated, Ellis picked up the ball and started running down the field.

Such a move was against the rules, and Ellis was severely berated. His schoolmates, however, liked the idea of running with the ball. It took a while, but eventually this version of the game caught on. By 1846, it was legal to run with the ball in a game of "rugby," or "rugger." (The name William Webb Ellis soon became synonymous with nonconformity. He eventually "became a London clergyman and rector of St. Clement Dan's in the Strand."[6])

For a long time, the new sport was played strictly in schools. By 1871, however, enough amateur clubs were playing to warrant the formation of the Rugby Football Union. Rugby is still enjoyed by millions of English youngsters today. It spread to America—as did "rounders," baseball's ancestor—in the nineteenth century.

Meanwhile, the original version of the game, which disallowed running with the ball, had also become more formalized. The Football Association was formed in a London tavern in 1863 to establish a uniform set of rules for the pastime. The sport became

A nineteenth-century illustration of students playing rugby at the Rugby School in England.

12

CALCIO IN COSTUME

Calcio is the name by which soccer is known in Italy. One variation, first played in Florence, is called Calcio in Costume. This version likely originated in military encampments hundreds of years ago. Rather than a sport, it was a method of training men in martial combat.

The most famous match took place on February 17, 1530, in Piazza Santa Croce. The imperial armies of Pope Clement VII had attacked Florence the previous summer. The fighting spirit of the Florentine youths kept the enemy at bay for several months. The game was played that February, not just to continue the tradition of playing during the celebrations that preceded Lent, but also to show the city's contempt for the surrounding troops. Although the match was a success, the city eventually yielded to the imperial forces.

Today, matches are held between local teams each June. The contest, which is a mixture of soccer, rugby, and football, is played with participants dressed in fifteenth-century costumes. It is considered the highlight of the Florentine summer season.

Fans watch the opening ceremony of a game of Calcio in Costume in Florence.

known as "association football," except in the United States, where it was called "soccer," an abbreviated form of "association."

American college athletes took up a game similar to rugby in the early part of the nineteenth century. In 1827, students at Harvard University in Cambridge, Massachusetts, began what was to become an annual tradition. On the first Monday of the school year, the school's best athletes took part in a game called "ballown" that was played with very few restrictions. The contest was nothing less than all-out war and resulted in countless injuries and much spilt blood. "Bloody Monday" was soon duplicated at

several other Eastern universities. The excessive violence of the game, however, caused most competitions to be banned by 1860.

Two years later, the first formal football (soccer) association in the United States—the Oneida Football Club of Boston—was founded by seventeen-year-old Gerritt Smith Miller of the Epes Sargent Dixwell Private Latin School. The club was organized to allow alumni of the school to continue playing the game after they had graduated and was the first to have organized practices and assigned positions. Playing their games on a 100-yard-long by 50-yard-wide field on the

The Rutgers and Princeton football teams, shown here competing in 1914, played what is considered the first intercollegiate game in 1869.

Boston Common, the Oneidas went four years without tasting defeat.

As the rules for both soccer and rugby became more formalized, changes came about. Americanized football became a mixture of the two games, with rules varying slightly from school to school.

The First College Game

In New Jersey, Princeton and Rutgers became rivals because of their proximity to each other. It seemed only natural that the schools would continue their rivalry on the football field. On November 6, 1869, Princeton traveled to New Brunswick where the two teams met in what is considered the first intercollegiate football game. The contest was played using the modified London Football Association rules established in 1863. The object of the game was to kick a round inflated English soccer ball across the opponent's goal line, between two stakes that were set twenty-five feet apart. Running with the ball was not allowed. Players had to either kick it or hit it with their head. Each goal counted as one point.

Each team fielded twenty-five players. Two from each side, selected as captains, took their positions in front of the opposition's goal. The remaining players were separated into groups of "fielders" and "bulldogs." The fielders were assigned to patrol particular areas of the field, which they were not allowed to leave; the bulldogs could go anywhere on the field. To distinguish between the two teams, many of the

Rutgers players wore red scarves or stocking caps on their heads. Because of this, the team became known as the Scarlet Knights, a nickname which has stuck to the present day.

A major difference between this game and soccer was the American innovation of blocking, or interference. Teammates of the player controlling the ball formed a wall in front of him and tried to push their opponents out of the way. Not even rugby made allowances for this new wrinkle.

As approximately one hundred spectators looked on, Rutgers scored first and held off their larger opponents, eventually coming out on top by a score of 6-4. The next week, a rematch was held on Princeton's field with the home squad gaining a measure of revenge with an 8-0 victory. A third game was also scheduled, but was called off when the administrations of both schools agreed that the contests were interfering with the players' studies.

Within a couple of years, Columbia, Yale, Cornell, Stevens Technical, New York University, City College of New York, and Harvard formed teams. In 1873, several of these schools formed the first intercollegiate football association. Harvard, the most prestigious university in the country, was invited to join the others but declined because of a basic difference in its game: In the Harvard version (known as the "Boston game"), a player was allowed to run with the ball if he was pursued by the opposition. Stopping the forward movement of a player by knocking

him down or tackling him was also acceptable.

Early the next year, the rugby team from McGill University in Montreal, Canada, came to Cambridge to play a two-game series against Harvard's football team. The first contest was played on May 14 under Harvard's rules, with the Massachusetts school winning by a score of 3-0. The second game, played under the rules of rugby that allowed a player to grab the ball and run with it at any time, ended in a scoreless tie. Harvard came away from the series with a high respect for the Canadians' game. The Harvard players liked the fast-moving action that featured lateral passes, bone-crunching tackles, an unusual prolate (elongated or egg-shaped) ball, and "touchdowns," whereby a ball carrier crossed the opponent's goal line.

Although no one realized it at the time, the game heralded a turning point in the history of football. In 1875, Harvard challenged Yale to a contest. The two teams agreed to use special rules: Harvard was allowed to run the ball, but Yale was not. The Elis, as the Yale players were known, came out on the short end of a 4-0 score, but like the Harvard players before them, found the running game to their liking. So, too, in short order, did the teams from Princeton and Columbia. The next year, representatives from the four schools met in Springfield, Massachusetts, to form the American Intercollegiate Foot-Ball Association, a predecessor of the National Collegiate Athletic

Association. The meeting, which took place at a hotel in Springfield called the Massasoit House, is sometimes referred to as "the Massasoit convention."

While there, the representatives reached an agreement on the first set of rules for American football (at the time called rugby football). The schools began with the standard Rugby Union Code and then adapted it to their needs. Among other things, the rules stipulated that teams were to be made up of fifteen players. (Since Yale preferred the eleven-man game, it declined to join the new organization but agreed to play association members.) The game was divided into two 45-minute halves and played on a field 140 yards long by 70 yards wide. There was no need for an end zone beyond the goal line because passing was not allowed. Touchdowns, scored when a player carrying the ball crossed the opponent's goal line, were worth one point each. Goals kicked from the field were worth four points. Such goals had to pass over a rudimentary crossbar, which was usually a clothesline stretched taut between two poles.

Play began with the kicking team lining up at the field's center line. The kicker could either punt, drop-kick, place-kick, or dribble the ball toward the receiving team. He could also fake a kick by tapping the ball, picking it up, and either running with it or lateraling it to a teammate.

When the player with the ball was downed, the next play began with what is known in rugby as a "scrum," or "scrummage." The ball was placed on the ground with members of both teams gathered around it. The players would push and shove each other until the ball was kicked free. A player could then pick it up and begin heading toward the goal line. If he was trapped and unable to continue forward, he might lateral the ball to a teammate or kick it downfield. If the other team got possession, the action progressed in the other direction.

From this crude beginning, the American game of football gradually began to take form.

Walter Camp, the "Father of American Football"

One of the stars of the Yale team was a young man named Walter Chauncey Camp from New Haven, Connecticut. Camp was a magnificent runner and kicker from the halfback position. He was captain of the team, which at that time was equivalent to being head coach. Because of the eligibility rules of the day, he played six years for the Elis, during which time the team won twenty-five games, lost one, and tied six. Camp also competed in baseball, track (some credit him with being the first to run over hurdles rather than to jump over them), tennis, swimming, rowing, and gymnastics, but football was the game with which he became infatuated.

Camp was a heroic figure at the school. He believed in values everyone could appreciate. "There is no substitute for hard work and effort beyond the call of mere duty," he would say. "That is what strengthens the soul and ennobles one's character."[7]

Camp attended Yale Medical School for two years, but left before getting his degree to work in his uncle's business, the New Haven Clock Company. He did not give up his association with football, however. He became an adviser at Yale in 1888 and soon dominated the athletic department. Rather than taking an active role on the field, he imparted his wisdom through his coaches. "His advice had authority because it was good advice," explained former Yale player and coach Tad Jones. "The practice then was to have the former year's captain return as head coach, and Camp, by serving every year as adviser, gave unity and continuity to these shifting assistants."[8]

In 1889, Camp and his friend Caspar Whitney, part owner of a magazine called *This Week's Sport*, picked the first All-American team. The two probably collaborated in choosing the annual team, a list of their choices for the best players at each position, through 1896. After that, the selections were published under Camp's name, mostly in *Collier's* magazine, through 1924. A player could receive no greater honor than to be named to one of those teams.

Camp's greatest contributions to the game he loved, however, were improvements to rules. As captain of the team, Camp represented Yale at the annual rules convention as a sophomore in 1877. He at-

Walter Chauncey Camp proposed guidelines that helped improve the game of football.

tended every succeeding one up to his death in 1925. (Ironically, he died while attending a rules meeting in New York City.)

Without Camp's assistance, it is questionable whether football would have made it into the twentieth century. The game often deteriorated into a boring contest of endless scrums, with large bodies elbowing and bulldozing against one another trying to gain an advantage that might eventually lead to a score. Camp proposed guidelines that helped alter the face of the game. As famous football coach and historian Parke Davis stated, "What Washington was to his country, Camp was to American football—the friend, the founder, and the father."[9]

CHAPTER 2

Playing the Game

ANY OF THE differences which distinguish football from rugby and soccer came about through the suggestions and proposals of Walter Camp. His contributions to the game cannot be overstated.

Transforming the Game

Camp's fascination with football caused numerous changes in the way the game was played. Among the first of these were his suggestions to reduce the number of players per side from fifteen to eleven and the size of the field to 110 yards (ten more than the current length) by 53 yards (one foot narrower than at present). The Intercollegiate Foot-Ball Association adopted these guidelines in 1880.

Until that year, football plays began with a scrummage. Camp's idea, also passed by

the convention, was to allow one team to maintain possession until it voluntarily turned over the ball to its opponent when it could not make further headway. If a player was stopped, or tackled, the next play began with a snap from the "snapper-back." At first this move was made with the foot. The snapper-back pressed down on the ball with his foot, sending it rolling into the backfield. This move eventually evolved into the snap with the hands that we know today. A play that began this way was known as a scrimmage.

The only flaw in Camp's plan was due to a mistake in judgment. Teams refused to voluntarily surrender the ball; instead they held onto it for an entire half of play. The other team would then do the same in the second half in what became known as the "block game."

To solve the problem, Camp suggested that a team be forced to give up the ball if it could not move it forward within a certain number of plays. In 1882, a rule was passed giving a team three chances, or "downs," to advance the ball five yards. This was later increased to ten yards. The result of these rule changes was that strategy and set plays became an important part of the game. Player positions and roles, therefore, had to become better defined.

The forward line consisted of seven players, called "forwards" or "rushers," stationed several feet apart from each other. Since the snapper-back was usually in the middle of the seven, he became known as the "center." The players on either side who guarded the center became known as "guards." The next players in line were the ones with the best chance of making tackles, giving them their names, while the players at the end of the line were simply called "ends." The linemen's main job was to move their defensive counterparts out of the way so that the man with the ball could gain yardage.

The player who received the snap, called the "quarterback" because of his position a quarter of the way back behind the line, was responsible for calling the signals for the play to be run. This usually meant nothing more than deciding which hole in the line a player would run through. The quarterback could not run with the ball himself or throw it forward. He handed it off to one of two "halfbacks," or the "fullback," so called because they lined up, respectively, either halfway or fully back behind the line. If the ball carrier saw he could not make further progress, he might kick the ball over the heads of the opposing players.

Set plays became an important part of football in the late nineteenth century.

This move had two possible benefits: first, it might push the opposing team back, deep into its own territory; second, since either team could recover a kick this move gave the offensive side a chance to make a big gain on the play. Despite a limited repertoire of plays, Camp still understood the importance of the man who took the snap. In his 1886 book, *Foot Ball: How to Coach a Team,* Camp explained the quarterback's responsibilities. "If he executes his part of the play," wrote Camp, "and the rest of it fails, he must receive the blame. . . . Place plenty of reliance upon him, but let him understand that this reliance necessitates his knowing everything that is transpiring as well as making some use of that knowledge."[10]

When a team got close to the opposition's goal line, it might attempt a "field goal." A field goal was a dropkick that went between the goal posts, which stood eighteen-and-a-half feet apart, with a crossbar ten feet high. A dropkick was made when a player dropped the ball with the point facing down. It was kicked just as it rebounded off the ground. This kind of kick could be made from anywhere on the field, at any time. Better players were able to execute it while running toward the goal line.

In the game's early years, a touchdown was worth one point, while a field goal was worth four. Complaints about scoring arose when a team claimed that one kick was more difficult than another. In addition, points scored on touchdowns were harder won, and

therefore deemed to be of more value than points scored on a field goal, yet field goals were worth more.

Camp responded to these complaints with a new scoring system in 1883. A field goal was set at five points, a goal kicked after a touchdown at four, a touchdown at two, and a safety (when a team was stopped behind its own goal line) at one. Previously, no points had been awarded for a safety. It would still be some time before the present values for touchdowns and field goals were implemented. A touchdown increased to five points in 1897, with a goal after reduced to one. A field goal was decreased to four points in 1904, then to three points five years later. In 1912, a touchdown became six points.

As the nineteenth century came to a close, the game had clearly broken away from soccer and rugby. Football, as we know it, was beginning to emerge. But the game was also becoming more violent. Players were larger and bulkier. The physical contact became extreme, leading to more frequent—and more serious—injuries. This trend threatened the future of what had become the most popular sport on college campuses around the country.

Bigger and Stronger Players

Blocking began to play a more important role as football entered the 1880s. Originally, the offsides rule found in rugby was followed in football. This meant that no team-

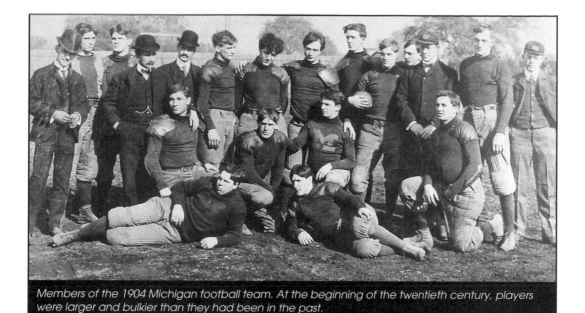

Members of the 1904 Michigan football team. At the beginning of the twentieth century, players were larger and bulkier than they had been in the past.

mate could run ahead of the player with the ball. By the end of the decade, however, this guideline was largely ignored.

In 1888, a new rule legalized tackling from the waist to the knees. Offensive linemen were forced to line up in a crouching position in order to avoid having their legs cut from beneath them by charging defensive players. To make matters even more difficult, offensive linemen were banned from extending their arms to grab a defender or to shove him out of the way. Coaches had to come up with new plays to counteract the new restrictions.

In one variation, the offensive linemen moved closer together to put a barrier between the runner and the defensive team. Teams soon found that this was even more effective if the blocking linemen fell back to form a

protective "V" around the man with the ball. When the linemen linked arms and moved forward together as a single unit, the play was difficult to stop. This "V-trick," or "wedge" play, quickly became the play of choice for teams around the country.

A second strategy that proved effective was implemented by legendary coach, and former Yale star, Amos Alonzo Stagg. Stagg coached football at the college level for an incredible fifty-seven years. He is credited with pioneering numerous innovations on the gridiron, including the huddle, the T-formation (a formation in which the fullback stands directly behind the quarterback, with halfbacks on either side, thus giving the appearance of a "T"), the quick kick (a punt attempted on a first, second, or third down, intended to take the opposing team by surprise), the man-in-motion, numbers on uniforms, and padded goal posts. As the immortal player and coach Knute Rockne would say, "All football comes from Stagg."[11]

Stagg had his two ends drop back from the line of scrimmage. This enabled them to get a running start and to build up momentum in their struggle to block the defensive linemen. This strategy eventually led to more complex variations, because the ends did not limit themselves to plowing straight ahead. They might crisscross in the backfield or pull toward one side or the other in an attempt to spring the runner free.

Stagg devised many other plays in addition to "ends back." One of the most unusual and most copied was the "turtleback." When the ball was snapped, the offensive players formed a tight oval around the ball carrier. This oval would swing toward one side of the field and then unroll downfield, where each player would block an opponent.

The Flying Wedge

Soon after the wedge play came into fashion, a Boston businessman by the name of Lorin F. Deland (who never played football himself) came up with a new idea. He combined the V-shape of the wedge with the

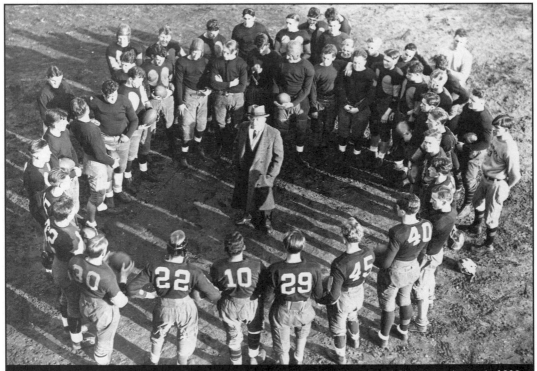
Coaching pioneer Amos Alonzo Stagg (center) addresses his University of Chicago players in 1939.

The Flying Wedge play was banned in 1893 because of the number of injuries it caused.

running start of the ends back. The result was the most famous play of all, the "Flying Wedge." He mentioned the play to the captain of the Harvard team, who first used it in his school's game against Yale. This play nearly brought about football's demise.

Harvard first used the Flying Wedge for kickoff plays in 1892. The players arranged themselves in two lines across the field. When the captain gave the signal, the players raced toward the ball at full speed, formed a wedge around the ball carrier, and plowed their way down the field. The play usually gained a good bit of yardage, with opposing players being left behind in its wake.

Not surprisingly, the number of football injuries soared as more and more teams began using the play. This number increased even further when schools applied the idea of having blockers take a running start when-

ever possible, on every type of play. Coach George W. Woodruff of the University of Pennsylvania is usually credited with being one of the first to make use of this principle.

In 1893, several new rules were passed to make the game safer. All variations of the wedge were banned, as was the practice of tackling players other than the ball carrier. The kickoff play was changed significantly. No longer could the kicking team retain possession by tapping the ball lightly and then running with it. Now the ball had to be kicked to give the other team a chance to receive it. Other changes shortened the length of a game from ninety minutes to seventy minutes and added a third official to help control play on the field. Previously, there had only been a referee, whose job it was to follow the movement of the ball, and an umpire, who was responsible for spotting infractions.

As has always been the case, however, the more inventive coaches soon came up with ways to get around the new regulations. Many squads moved some of their biggest linemen into the backfield where a running start gave them a tremendous advantage when blocking opposing players. Injury levels remained high. By 1904, several colleges dropped football altogether. The game's future did not look bright.

Theodore Roosevelt Steps In

In 1905, eighteen college players died on the field of play, with 148 others incurring serious injuries. The senseless brutality that had taken over the game outraged more and

Theodore Roosevelt threatened to abolish football if changes weren't made to discourage foul play and brutality.

more people. Among these was President Theodore Roosevelt.

Roosevelt called together representatives from Harvard, Princeton, and Yale, and laid down the law. Unless significant changes were made, he would abolish the sport of football once and for all by pushing for legislation to make it illegal. "Brutality and foul play," said the president, "should receive the same summary punishment given to a man who cheats at cards."[12] Soon after, representatives from more than sixty schools met to plan the sport's future. Out of the meeting the Intercollegiate Athletic Association (IAA), which later changed its name to the National Collegiate Athletic Association (NCAA), was formed.

With Walter Camp once again at the forefront, new guidelines were established in 1906. Requirements for retaining possession of the ball changed. The number of yards needed to gain a "first down" was raised from five to ten. This resulted in fewer straight-ahead runs, since crashing into the line rarely resulted in large gains. The game opened up, becoming less restrained by set patterns, which made it more interesting to watch.

A narrow neutral zone the length of a football was set up between the opposing lines. All linemen were required to take their positions on—rather than behind—the line, ending the practice of getting running starts. The length of the game was shortened even further to sixty minutes and another official was added to help control play.

The forward pass was legalized to open up the game and to lessen the advantage held by the teams with the biggest players.

The Forward Pass

What would ultimately prove to be the most important new rule of all, however, received little immediate attention. To open up the game even more—and to lessen the advantage held by teams with the biggest players—the forward pass was made legal. The ball could not be thrown directly over the center, however; it had to be passed at least five yards to the right or left of where it had been snapped. To help officials determine if the five-yard rule had been followed, stripes five yards apart were drawn lengthwise down the field, giving it a checkerboard appearance. This gave rise to the term "gridiron" in referring to the field of play.

Despite the obvious advantages of the pass (the ball could be thrown over the linemen, avoiding contact with them altogether), teams were slow to add it to their arsenals for several reasons. First, the ball was much wider than the modern one, making it more difficult to grasp and throw accurately. Second, and perhaps most important, was a key difference in the rules of the day. Many years later, Michigan State head coach Duffy Daugherty explained his adherence to the running game: "Only three things can happen when you put a ball up in the air—and two of them are bad [an interception or an incomplete pass]."[13] This was even more true in 1906. At that time, an incomplete pass was considered a live ball.

FOOTBALL INVENTIONS

Like every other sport, football has seen its share of innovations through the years, many in the area of equipment. Practice field devices, such as the blocking sled and tackling dummy, are standard trappings at every level from high school through the pros. Some other devices, however, have met with less than enthusiastic approval.

In 1933, for example, two gentlemen from Kentucky received a patent for an antifumble football. Their invention had sand glued into grooves which ran the length of the ball. Theoretically, the ball would be easier to hold onto. Players, however, disagreed. It proved to be just about as popular as the 1969 water-holding antifumble football patented by Albert Russo of Virginia. This spheroid was filled with water that shifted around as the ball was carried. When used in practice, the ball required a player to grip it more tightly, hopefully developing a habit that would carry over into the game. Another practice device had a football attached to the wrist by a tether that snapped the ball back to the thrower, allowing him to practice his art by himself.

The goalposts have also been the object of innovation. A 1958 patent was awarded for a graded-scoring structure, which consisted of four posts and two crosspieces. Different point values were to be awarded for kicks of varying levels of difficulty. Another inventor had himself, more than the players, in mind. Unable to see from the far end of the field during night games, Nick Zapos designed light-up goal posts that could be activated by the referee with the touch of a button.

Either team could pick it up and run with it, just like with a fumble.

The first college team to incorporate the pass into its offense to a significant degree was St. Louis University, under coach Eddie Cochems, in 1906. As Cochems explained, "[I saw] the seven lacings as the only physical part of the ball for finger purchase [grip] in throwing [it] on its long axis. . . . I told the players to put their fingers between the two lacings nearest the end of the ball, where the diameter was the shortest, and throw it with a twist of the wrist."[14]

St. Louis probably first used the pass in a game against Carroll College played in early September, with quarterback Brad Robinson throwing to teammate Jack Schneider. St. Louis went undefeated that season, outscoring its opponents by 402 points to 11. At the University of Chicago, Amos Alonzo Stagg began diagraming passing plays, many of which are still used today.

Further rule changes encouraged usage of the pass. In 1910, one directive forbade the defensive team from hitting or tackling a receiver while the ball was in the air. Two years later, offenses were given a fourth down in which to try to advance ten yards, making it less of a gamble to try to pass on at least one of the plays. Another rule allowed a receiver to catch the ball past the goal line for a touchdown, rather than having to run the ball over as had been required previously. Thus, the end zone came into existence.

Despite these measures, colleges still used the pass sparingly. More experimentation was taking place at the high school level. Not until quarterback Charles "Gus" Dorais and end Knute Rockne teamed up at Notre Dame University in 1913 did colleges see how devastating a good passing game could be.

At the time Rockne enrolled, Notre Dame was a relatively small school with a student body of about five hundred. Most of the college's athletic competitions were against other small schools. An exception was made in 1913, however, when a football match was scheduled against the United States Military Academy, or Army.

Army had one of the top teams in the country, and no one gave the team from South Bend, Indiana, any chance for victory. What Army did not know, however, was that teammates Dorais and Rockne, at the suggestion of coach Jesse Harper, had spent the previous summer working on their throwing and catching skills. When the 1913 season began, Notre Dame opened with three lopsided victories—87-0 over Ohio Northern, 20-7 over North Dakota, and 62-0 over Alma. The November 1 contest against Army would be the ultimate test.

With the game scoreless midway through the opening quarter, Dorais and Rockne connected on a forty-yard pass for the game's first score. Army fought back to take a one-point lead at the half, but the Notre Dame attack was unlike any they had seen

before. Dorais was magnificent, completing fourteen of seventeen passes for 243 yards. Rockne's receptions hurt Army time and time again. By the time the final gun had sounded, Notre Dame was on the front end of a 35-13 score. As the *New York Times* gushed, "The Westerners flashed the most sensational football that has been seen in the East this year, baffling the cadets with a style of open play and a perfectly developed forward pass, which carried the victors

Notre Dame end Knute Rockne devastated opponents with his pass receptions.

HELMETS

When Princeton and Rutgers took the field for the first intercollegiate football game in 1869, the only equipment used was a soccer ball. Nothing distinguishes today's players from those of yesteryear more than the uniforms and protective equipment that they wear. Perhaps surprisingly, the piece of equipment players accepted last was the helmet. It was not until 1943 that the NFL made such protection mandatory.

The first version of football headgear was a leather head harness, which came into use around the turn of the century. Fitting tightly against the skull, the harness provided little actual protection. Helmets began to appear some twenty years later. A web suspension system kept the skull away from the helmet shell.

By the late 1930s, a fiber shell with sponge-rubber padding had replaced the leather helmet. Soon after, the John T. Riddell Company patented a molded plastic helmet. This was a crucial turning point, because the plastic was clearly superior to the earlier materials. It became the standard model following World War II.

Face masks began to be used more often around the same time. A single-bar face mask made its first appearance during the 1930s. It gained acceptance following the war, but did not become mandatory until the 1950s. The bar tubular mask, in which a bar of rubber and plastic provided protection for the face, was originally designed for Cleveland Browns quarterback Otto Graham. It eventually led to the double-bar, triple-bar, and bird-cage varieties worn by modern-day players.

down the field thirty yards at a clip."[15] The effectiveness of the passing game had been dramatically demonstrated at the college level.

Fine-Tuning the Game

The game that Dorais and Rockne played, for the most part, is the same one played today. Further rule changes made the game safer for the participants. In 1914, for example, a rule was instituted that penalized players for "roughing the passer." Eighteen years later, players were prohibited from striking an opponent above the shoulders. The following year, colleges encouraged players to wear leather helmets for protection. Helmets were not made compulsory, however, until 1939. It would be another thirty-four years before mouth protectors were also mandated.

Equipment has also changed. The football itself has been streamlined to make it easier to handle and throw. The goalposts were moved to the rear of the end zone in 1927. The distance between the posts was widened by almost five feet in 1959, before being reduced to its original eighteen feet, six inches in 1991.

The changes in rules produced a more entertaining game on the field. Off the field, the game was undergoing another significant transformation. Money became a factor that could not be ignored.

CHAPTER 3

The Pros
Take the Field

UNLIKE PROFESSIONAL BASEBALL, professional football took a good while to catch on with the public. Most fans believed that players representing their school played with more pride and greater intensity than did those whose only interest was money. As late as the mid-1920s, many agreed with the opinion expressed by John L. Griffith, head of the Big Ten collegiate football conference: "The college spirit is lacking in professional football," he said. "The players are not willing to risk injury just to enable an outstanding star to make a good showing."[16] It would only be a matter of time, however, before the pro version of the game took hold.

The First Pros

It is likely that the first players to receive some sort of compensation for playing foot-ball were college players in the late 1880s. The first documented evidence, however, points to the year 1892. At that time, football

Most early-twentieth-century football fans believed that college players (pictured) played with more intensity and pride than professionals.

had become popular with the athletic clubs found in many cities. The first was the New York Athletic Club, which opened its doors in 1868. Former college players who wished to continue playing the game joined these associations, where they also had the opportunity to develop business contacts.

The rules dealing with amateurism dictated that players for these clubs were not to receive payment for their services, but some teams used ingenious methods of getting

Yale standout guard William W. "Pudge" Heffelfinger.

around those rules. In 1890, the Orange Athletic Club of New Jersey rewarded the best players with trophies or watches at the end of the season. The players would visit a local pawnbroker who might give them $20 for the item. The player then sold the pawn ticket to the team manager for another $20, and the manager bought the watch back from the broker, making the gift available to be given out once again. The player was $40 richer, while still maintaining his amateur status. Eventually, the awarding of trophies was banned by the Amateur Athletic Union (AAU), which had been formed in 1888 to protect the sport from such shenanigans.

Still, despite the efforts of the AAU, some clubs persisted in violating the rules. Because of the competitive nature of the games, it was not unusual for some clubs to bring in "ringers" (star athletes who were not regular club members) to play in important contests. Historian Thomas Jable wrote, "As competition increased in intensity and winning became important, the athletic club turned to the established athlete from the outside. . . . In hiring the gifted player or professional, the athletic club shattered the amateur ideal upon which it was founded, that is, participation for the sheer love of the game."[17]

In western Pennsylvania, where club football was especially popular, two of the bitterest rivals were the Allegheny Athletic Association (AAA) and the Pittsburgh Athletic Club (PAC). When the two clubs met in November 1892, the star of the game was former Yale standout William W. "Pudge" Heffelfinger of the AAA. Heffelfinger was the most famous player of his time, as well as one of the largest. He stood six feet, three inches tall, and weighed just over 200 pounds. As a guard, he was named to the All-American team in 1889, 1890, and 1891. Among other things, he is credited with originating the move whereby the guard drops back and leads interference for the ball carrier. In the contest against the PAC, Heffelfinger scored the only points of the game when he picked up a fumble and rumbled thirty-five yards for a touchdown. The AAA won by a final score of 4-0. For his efforts in the game, Heffelfinger had his expenses paid. He also received the sum of $500 as a "performance bonus."[18]

Other teams in Pennsylvania also hired star players, among them the Greensburg Athletic Association which hired former Princeton star Lawton Fiscus, and a club in Latrobe which hired high school quarterback John Brallier. But the Amateur Athletic Union was determined to see that players on its teams were untainted by recompense of any sort, since paying players was clearly a violation of AAU rules. As a result, the organization conducted investigations into the hiring of amateur players. In 1896, the Allegheny Athletic Association was banished from the AAU for paying players. It decided to field a team that was openly professional, recruiting the best players available. Professional football was no longer a secret.

In 1893, the PAC signed at least one player to a formal contract. (Before that, there were no written agreements.) Although the paper on which it was written was torn across the signature, the player referred to in this first-ever player contract is believed to have been halfback Grant Dibert. The agreement stated, "I hereby agree to participate in all regularly scheduled football games of the Pittsburg (sic) Athletic Club for the full season of 1893. As an active player I agree to accept a salary of $50 per contest and also acknowledge that I will play for no other club during PAC games."[19]

The First Pro League

The Pittsburgh Athletic Club was only one of a number of professional teams, including the Allegheny Athletic Association, Duquesne Country and Athletic Club, Greensburg Athletic Association, and Latrobe Athletic Club, that flourished in the late 1890s in and around the Pittsburgh region, occasionally drawing crowds of more than 10,000 to their games. When the Duquesne club found itself in financial difficulties, sportsman William Chase Temple took over the payments. He thus became, unofficially, the first individual owner of a professional football team.

In 1902, the owners of three major league baseball teams became involved in football. Pittsburgh Pirates owner Barney Dreyfus put his money behind the Pittsburgh Stars franchise, a club founded by Latrobe newspaperman David J. Berry. One

GEORGIA TECH 222, CUMBERLAND 0

When tiny Cumberland College of Lebanon, Tennessee, traveled to Atlanta, Georgia, to take on powerful Georgia Tech on October 7, 1916, they had few hopes of victory. In reality, Cumberland kept the date at Tech's Grant Field only because, due to an earlier agreement between the teams, they stood to forfeit $3,000 if they failed to field a team. What befell Cumberland, however, could not have been imagined in their worst nightmares.

Coach John Heisman's Tech squad administered the most lopsided defeat in college football annals. They jumped out to a 63-0 lead after just one period of play, then added 63 more points in the second quarter to lead 126-0 at the half. By the time the annihilation had ended, Cumberland was on the short end of a 222-0 score.

Tech had thirty-two possessions in the game and scored touchdowns on every one. The Ramblin' Wreck, as Tech was known, did not attempt a single pass all game, scoring nineteen times on twenty-nine rushes. They gained 501 yards on the ground, or 17.3 per carry. They also scored touchdowns on five of six interception returns, five of nine punt returns, two of three fumble-recovery returns, and one of five kickoff returns.

Things got so bad for Cumberland, they began kicking off after Tech touchdowns instead of receiving (as allowed by the rules of the day) in hopes of pinning Tech deep in its own territory. Nothing worked, however. Perhaps the ultimate indignity occurred in the third period. Running out of players, Cumberland coach George Allen inserted himself in the game to punt. Allen's kick struck his own center squarely in the back of the head.

of Pittsburgh's best-known players was fullback/punter Christy Mathewson, a pitcher with the National League's New York Giants.

Philadelphia Athletics manager and owner Connie Mack organized a football team that included his star pitcher, Rube Waddell. It is likely that Waddell was only on the squad so Mack could keep tabs on the eccentric hurler during the off-season. Philadelphia Phillies owner Art Rogers also fielded a team. In September 1902, Berry announced the formation of a new organization which consisted of the Stars, Athletics, and Phillies. Berry himself was named president of the circuit. The loose confederation had no bylaws and allowed each club to make up its own schedule.

This early professional football league lasted only one season. Since each team played a different number of games, there was a question as to who was the league champion. The Phillies split four league games on their way to an overall record of 8-3. The Athletics won three, lost two, and tied one within the league, and were 10-2-2 overall. The Stars compiled a 9-2-1 mark against all comers, and 2-2-1 in the league. The Stars and Athletics met in a championship game before eighteen hundred fans, but the contest ended in a scoreless tie. In a rematch two days later, the Stars came out on top by a score of 11-0.

In 1902, the Athletics also played the first professional night contest. The Philadelphia club traveled to Elmira, New York, where they routed the Kanaweola Cycle Club by a score of 39-0. Most likely, huge searchlights stationed near each end zone illuminated the field.

The short-lived league had little success at the gate. Others, however, felt the game could still be an attraction if promoted in the right way.

The Football "World Series"

Late December was not a busy time of the year for New York City's Madison Square Garden, at least until college basketball began to catch on with the fans. To attract some business, Tom O'Rourke, manager of the Garden, decided to stage a tournament among some of football's top teams of 1902. He invited several college and professional clubs, but many turned him down for a variety of reasons. The five who accepted the invitations were the Knickerbocker Athletic Club and the Warlow Athletic Club from New York, the Orange (N.J.) Athletic Club, the Syracuse (N.Y.) Athletic Club, and an all-star team simply called the New Yorks.

The forty-minute games in the three-day tournament were played on a seventy-yard-long by thirty-five-yard-wide field. When all was said and done, the Syracuse squad proved victorious, defeating the New Yorks, the Knickerbocker Athletic Club, and the Orange Athletic Club on successive nights.

Despite limited success (crowds averaged 2,500 per night), the tournament was staged again the following year. One of the clubs that accepted an invitation in 1903 was an all-star team from Franklin, Pennsylvania. Local promoter Billy Prince, who had signed many top players, put together the Franklin team. His squad stood head and shoulders above every other team in western Pennsylvania. They played their entire 1903 schedule without suffering a single defeat, or being scored upon.

At the tournament in Madison Square Garden, Franklin demonstrated its dominance. It defeated the Red and Blacks of the Watertown (N.Y.) Athletic Association, 12-0, to take the second—and last—football "world series." Low attendance convinced O'Rourke to abandon his experiment. Although the concept of the series did not stick with football, baseball successfully adopted the idea.

Ironically, Franklin's dominance eventually led to a shift of football's center from Pennsylvania to northeastern Ohio. Several of the better Pennsylvania players who were not signed by Prince joined the 1903 Ohio state champion Massillon Tigers squad, which took the championship again the next year. This prompted the nearby town of Canton, a long-time sports rival of Massillon,

Canton All-America halfback Willie Heston.

The Bulldogs responded by suggesting that the Tigers had begun the rumor to hurt attendance at Canton's games. Whether the rumors were true or not is lost to history. The result was that both teams suffered at the gate. It would be several years before the rivalry again reached a fever pitch.

The person who eventually rekindled the rivalry was former Carlisle Indian School standout Jim Thorpe. In 1915, Canton owner Jack Cusack signed Thorpe to play for $250 per game. Thorpe was the greatest all-around player of the day. In addition to being a battering ram of a runner, he could punt, drop-kick and place-kick, block, and play defense. Besides sparking the Bulldogs with his play, Thorpe boosted attendance with his drawing power. Interest in professional football, which had been on the wane in Ohio since the gambling rumors, perked up once again as Canton dominated the loose alliance known as the Ohio League from 1916 to 1919.

George Halas and the American Professional Football Association

Following a temporary lull during World War I when many star players were serving with the military, pro ball experienced another surge in interest. Powerful teams flourished as far west as Wisconsin. One of these teams—the Hammond (Ind.) Pros—featured an end by the name of George Halas, often referred to today as the "father of

to form its own team, the Bulldogs. The rivalry sparked a bidding war between the two teams for the best players. As a result, salaries increased significantly. One Canton player, All-America halfback Willie Heston, was paid $600 for one game against Massillon, surpassing the $500 paid to Pudge Heffelfinger.

However, an unfortunate side effect of the higher level of play was an increase in the amount of money wagered on the contests. In 1906, Massillon coach Ed Stewart, who was also city editor of the *Massillon Independent,* accused Canton of trying to bribe Massillon players to throw a game.

the NFL." In addition to starring on the gridiron, Halas had been captain of the University of Illinois basketball team and also an excellent baseball player. He played right field with the New York Yankees until a young slugger by the name of Babe Ruth beat him out of a job.

In 1920, Halas left Hammond to take a job with the Staley Starchworks in Decatur, Illinois. The company's owner, A. E. Staley, believed that fielding a winning sports team would generate publicity and business for the firm and hired Halas to help him accomplish this goal. "I was elated," said Halas. "I saw the offer as an exciting opportunity, but did not suspect the tremendous future Mr. Staley was opening for me."[20] Staley offered players a regular job and a percentage of gate receipts, which helped Halas convince several of the region's top athletes to sign with the company.

In late summer of 1920, Canton Bulldogs manager Ralph E. Hay, contacted Halas. Hay, a twenty-nine-year-old Hupmobile auto dealer in Canton, told Halas of a meeting that had taken place in his office on August 20. Representatives from teams in Akron, Canton, Cleveland, and Dayton had discussed the possibility of forming a new professional football league. *The Canton Evening Repository* reported that plans for the American Professional Football Conference emerged from the meeting. Hay was instructed to contact representatives of other strong clubs and invite them to a sec-

ond meeting. Halas was one of those invited.

On September 17, 1920, Halas and the managers of nine other pro teams met at Hay's dealership to discuss plans for the league. Since Hay's office was too small for the gathering, the men congregated on the auto showroom floor. Halas later recalled, "We only had two chairs at that meeting. Everybody else sat on the runningboards or the fenders."[21]

The meeting resulted in the establishment of the ten-team American Professional Football Association (APFA). The

Canton Bulldog Jim Thorpe increased attendance with his superb all-around play.

association's purpose was "to raise the standard of professional football in every way possible, to eliminate bidding for players between rival clubs and to secure cooperation in the formation of schedules."[22] To give the league instant credibility, Jim Thorpe, the most famous player of the day, was named honorary president.

Fourteen teams competed that first season. They were the Akron Pros, Buffalo All-Americans, Canton Bulldogs, Chicago Racine Cardinals, Chicago Tigers, Cleveland Tigers, Columbus Panhandles, Dayton Triangles, Decatur Staleys, Detroit Heralds, Hammond Pros, Muncie Flyers, Rochester Jeffersons, and Rock Island Independents. (The Buffalo All-Americans, Chicago Tigers, Columbus Panhandles, and Detroit Heralds were not charter members, but joined the league later.) On October 3, 1920, the hometown Dayton club defeated Columbus, 14-0, in the first league game. Lou Partlow of the Triangles ran for the league's first score.

Teams generally had sixteen-man rosters, with five substitutes joining the eleven starters. Most players played both offense and defense. Offenses were fairly conservative, despite the presence of many of the top stars of the day, which included Thorpe and Fritz Pollard, the first of the league's black stars. Most teams ran out of the single-wing alignment devised by Glenn "Pop" Warner of the Carlisle Indian School in 1906. Halas' Decatur Staleys were the only squad to use the radical T-formation. Passes were rare, with teams preferring to wait for the other club to make a mistake rather than chance one of their own.

No final standings for that first season were ever published. The teams had agreed to determine the champion by a vote of the members following the end of the season. In this way, teams that had scheduled easier opponents would not have an unfair advantage. On April 30, 1921, the Akron Pros were presented with the Brunswick-Balke Collender loving cup as the league's champion.

The APFA's first season was far from being a financial success. The average attendance at games was probably around 4,200. With stars earning around $150 per game, all the clubs lost money. The Muncie Flyers played just one game before closing shop; the Cleveland Tigers and Detroit Heralds called it quits soon after the season ended.

Nevertheless, the league managed to survive. The next two seasons brought several significant changes. The league expanded to twenty-one teams in 1921, with the Green Bay Packers among those joining. Most significant, Joseph F. Carr, manager of the Columbus Panhandles, was elected president, replacing Thorpe. Unlike Thorpe, Carr was an active, not simply honorary, president. He quickly established his authority and won the respect of the owners. Under his leadership, the APFA played its first organized season as a league, rather than as just a loose collec-

Joseph F. Carr (left) won the respect of team owners as president of the American Professional Football Association.

tion of teams. A league constitution, together with bylaws, was set down in writing. Schedules became more formalized, with league standings issued for the first time and games against nonleague teams not counted.

Halas' Staleys, now relocated in Chicago, were crowned league champions with a 10-1-1 record. (Due to poor business, Staley had informed Halas that the team would have to be dropped. He suggested Halas move it to Chicago and lent him money to get started. "All I ask," said Staley, "is that you continue to call the team the Staleys for one season."[23])

The Staleys changed their name to the Chicago Bears the following year when Halas and Dutch Sternaman became the official owners. In June, the APFA changed its name to the National Football League. A standard players' contract was established, which included a reserve clause similar to the one that baseball had adopted. This clause gave a club the rights to a player for an additional year if a new contract was not agreed upon by a specific date. Carr also appointed a committee to draft a new constitution that would govern the association. Although there had been many franchise shifts, professional football, as we know it, was at last beginning to set down roots.

The Barnstorming Bears

Despite Thorpe's presence, the professional football of the National Football League still did not garner as much attention as did the college game. Unpaid amateur stars who played for their love of the game were more attractive heroes than mercenaries who drew a salary for their efforts. Notre Dame, under Knute Rockne, became the glamour team of the early 1920s. The "Four Horsemen"—Elmer Layden, Jim Crowley, Don Miller, and Harry Stuhldreher—led the Fighting Irish to an undefeated season and national championship in 1924. All told, Rockne's clubs would win a total of 105 games against only twelve losses in his thirteen seasons at South Bend.

The greatest player of the era was running back Red Grange of the University of Illinois. Grange's exploits for the Illini electrified crowds wherever the team played. He was just what the NFL needed to assure its place as a major player on the sporting scene.

Two days after playing his last game for Illinois, Grange turned pro, against the wishes of his father. He had hired agent Charles C. Pyle to handle his affairs. C. C. Pyle, nicknamed "Cash and Carry," worked out a deal with the Chicago Bears that would pay Grange a large salary, as well as guarantee him 50 percent of all gate receipts. (Pyle would receive 40 percent of Grange's share.) Halas decided the deal was worth it to the team. As he saw it, "Pyle would provide Red; Red would provide the crowds; it was a fair arrangement."[24]

"The Four Horsemen," Notre Dame's formidable backfield. Left to right: Don Miller, Elmer Layden, Jim Crowley, and Harry Stuhldreher.

Grange played his first professional game against the Chicago Cardinals on Thanksgiving, less than a week after he had signed the contract. He played before 39,000 fans, the largest crowd ever to see an NFL game of any kind. Immediately afterward, with the approval of George Halas, Pyle arranged an eastern barnstorming tour in which the Bears would play ten games over seventeen days. The tour would feature both regular season and exhibition games.

The Bears played before 35,000 in Philadelphia on December 5, then broke the attendance record again when they entertained 73,000 in New York's Polo Grounds the next day. The $130,000 share taken in by Giants owner Tim Mara saved him from financial ruin. The huge crowds were changing perceptions about the sport. "All of a sudden," penned one Chicago writer, "some people around the country think that pro football might be a good investment."[25]

The Bears returned to Chicago to play the Giants in the final game of the tour on December 13. They then took an eight-day break before embarking on a second tour that Pyle had put together. The team traveled south to Coral Gables, Florida, on Christmas Day, then headed west. They set another attendance mark by drawing 75,000 in Los Angeles on January 16 before finishing up in Seattle on the last day of January.

Running back Red Grange's superior play sparked interest in the NFL.

During the two tours, Grange and the Bears played nineteen games in seventeen cities over the course of sixty-six days. More than 300,000 fans in all watched the Galloping Ghost (as Grange was called) perform his magic, earning him more than $200,000 in gate receipts, plus assorted endorsement fees. The money made Grange the wealthiest athlete in sports. Most important, he brought the National Football League the attention it needed to assure its survival.

In 1926, Pyle and Grange demanded from Halas a five-figure salary and part

THE 1932 NFL PLAYOFF GAME

In 1932, the Chicago Bears and Portsmouth Spartans ended the regular season with records of 6-1-6 and 6-1-4, respectively. Since ties were not counted in the standings, the two teams finished with the same mark. The league decided a play-off game would be held to determine the league champion.

Although the game was originally scheduled for Wrigley Field, bad weather caused it to be moved indoors to Chicago Stadium, where the teams met on December 18. The special playing conditions necessitated several new rules, including one that moved the ball laterally toward the center of the field when a play ended near the sidelines. This rule became the basis for the future introduction of hashmarks.

With no score in the fourth period, the Bears had a fourth-and-goal situation. Fullback Bronko Nagurski faked a plunge into the line, then stepped back and tossed a pass that Red Grange caught in the end zone for a touchdown. The rules of the day required a player to throw from at least five yards behind the line of scrimmage. Portsmouth coach George "Potsy" Clark argued that Nagurski had failed to do so. The score stood, however, and the Bears went on to post a 9-0 victory. The following year, largely because of the disputed play, the league passed a new rule: a pass could be thrown from anywhere behind the line of scrimmage.

ownership of the team. When Halas turned them down, Pyle leased Yankee Stadium and petitioned the league for a franchise. His request was refused, so he decided to form his own league. He founded the nine-team American Football League, with Grange as a member of the New York Yankees franchise. The ill-fated league survived just one season, however. The NFL allowed the Yankees to join the more-established league in 1927, but Grange suffered an injury in the third game of the year and never regained his former glory.

The 1930s

Football, like every other industry, was adversely affected by the Great Depression. Membership in the NFL dropped from a high of twenty-six teams in 1926 to twelve

in 1929, and finally to eight in 1932. Attendance fell at all levels, but interest in the game remained high. Both the pros and colleges adopted a new streamlined ball that made passing easier. Many teams opened up their game, following the example that Benny Friedman set in the late 1920s with the Cleveland Bulldogs, Detroit Wolverines, and New York Giants. Although Friedman's average of perhaps a dozen throws a game is not much by today's standards, it was a significant increase for his time. He could throw the ball on any down, from any part of the field. Defenses had to alter their plans of action, never knowing if Friedman was going to run or throw after getting the ball in the backfield.

Interest in the college game was sparked by a number of factors, including the increasing popularity of radio, the initiation of the Associated Press weekly rankings of the top teams, and the establishment of several new postseason bowl games. A fan could follow a team's games even when the players were on the road, could see how the team compared with other clubs around the country, and could hope for some measure of glory at the Rose Bowl, Orange Bowl, Sugar Bowl, Sun Bowl, or Cotton Bowl, even if a national championship was out of reach.

The top athletes from all over the country became national heroes. Tom Harmon, Don Hutson, Sammy Baugh, Whizzer White, and Nile Kinnick brought fame to their schools. They were admired by members of both sexes as the national media covered their accomplishments week after week.

In 1935, the Downtown Athletic Club in New York City awarded University of Chicago's Jay Berwanger a trophy for being the best player east of the Mississippi River. The following year, voting was expanded to include players from colleges all across the country. The trophy was named in honor of John Heisman, the club's athletic director and former head coach at Oberlin, Akron, Clemson, the University of Pennsylvania, Washington and Jefferson, Rice, and Georgia Tech. The Heisman Memorial Trophy has been awarded every year since then and has become, arguably, the most prestigious college award in any sport.

Coming of Age

As these new players entered the National Football League, they found several other

University of Wisconsin running back Ron Dayne poses with the Heisman Trophy, awarded every year to college football's best player.

changes that made the game more exciting. Passing rules were altered so that a player could throw the ball from anywhere behind the line of scrimmage. Previously, a player had to be at least five yards behind the line.

Another rule was instituted to spread the action over a greater portion of the field. Prior to 1933, the ball was placed where a runner or receiver was downed. If that happened to be near a sideline, the offense was forced to run a play toward the middle of the field. Defenses, therefore, tried to clog the middle and force play toward one of the sidelines.

To counteract this, two sets of hashmarks were marked off on the field, thirty feet in

THE ROSE BOWL

Bowl games are a part of football's long tradition. The oldest—the Rose Bowl—traces its ancestry back to 1902 when Stanford and Michigan met in a contest as part of the annual Tournament of Roses festivities in Pasadena, California. The game was not played again until 1916 when it became an annual event. It was christened the Rose Bowl in 1923.

Over the years, Pasadena has been the site of numerous outstanding individual and team performances. In 1925, the Four Horsemen of Notre Dame led the Irish to a 27-10 win over Stanford in their final collegiate appearance. In 1939, an unbeaten Duke team played the University of Southern California. Duke, which had not been scored upon all year, led 3-0 with less than one minute left in the game. Their unblemished season was ruined, however, when USC's fourth-string quarterback tossed a touchdown pass to give the Trojans a 7-3 win.

Perhaps the most famous Rose Bowl moment of all occurred in the 1929 game between California and Georgia Tech. With the score tied at 0-0, Tech fumbled at its own thirty-five-yard line. The ball was picked up by California's Roy Riegels, who had been running toward the sidelines. While pivoting to get away from a Georgia player, Riegels lost his bearings and began heading toward his own end zone. He was finally stopped by one of his teammates at the one-yard line, where he was downed by Tech players. California couldn't advance the ball, and when their attempted punt was blocked for a safety, Georgia gained a 2-0 lead. That safety turned out to be the difference, as Tech went on to win by a score of 8-7.

A capacity crowd watches the 1949 Rose Bowl.

from the sidelines. If a play ended near the sidelines, the ball was brought in to the hashmark on that side, giving the offense more room in which to maneuver.

Opening up the game in this way made passing a more attractive option. The newer ball, however, made kicking more difficult. In an attempt to reward kicking skills, the goal posts were moved up again to the goal line. The result was more field goals attempted and made, and fewer tie games.

A final change for the 1933 season was the separation of the league's ten teams into Eastern and Western divisions. The Eastern Division consisted of the Boston Redskins, Brooklyn Dodgers, New York Giants, Philadelphia Eagles, and Pittsburgh Pirates. The Western Division was made up of the Chicago Bears, Chicago Cardinals, Cincinnati Reds, Green Bay Packers, and Portsmouth Spartans.

The two division champions were to meet in the league's championship game, similar to baseball's World Series. In the first official championship match, the Western Division champion Chicago Bears defeated the Eastern Division titlist New York Giants by a score of 23-21. For their participation, each member of the winning Bears team received a bonus check for $210.23.

With a system now in place for postseason play, the league began another tradition. The following year, before the start of the regular season, the champion Bears played a team that comprised the top college play-

ers in the land in the first Chicago All-Star Game. The game was a resounding success. More than 79,000 fans turned out at Soldier Field in Chicago to watch the teams battle to a scoreless tie.

The college All-Stars had more luck with the Bears than did any of Chicago's regular-season opponents. The Bears compiled a perfect 13-0 mark and once again met the New York Giants in the championship game. The teams met at the Polo Grounds in New York City on a frigid, icy field on December 9, 1934.

With the Bears owning a 10-3 lead at halftime, the Giants decided to change from their football shoes into basketball sneakers for the second half to get better traction on the slippery field. They did so when the shoes arrived early in the third period. The sneakers did the trick. The Giants roared back with twenty-seven unanswered points in the last period and upset the mighty Bears, 30-13.

The Giants and Bears had clearly established themselves as the best teams of the National Football League. Afraid that such domination might hurt pro football's growing popularity, Philadelphia's Bert Bell made a proposal to bring about a measure of equality to the league. He suggested an annual draft of college players, with the first pick going to the team that finished last in the standings. The recommendation was approved, and the first NFL draft took place in 1936. Eventually, the draft did achieve its

NFL commissioner Paul Tagliabue (left) poses with a draft pick during the 2000 NFL Draft. The draft was first instituted in 1936 to promote parity among teams.

purpose, to the betterment of the league. As Halas explained, "Time proved that by leveling the clubs, the draft system heightened the attractiveness of the sport. It created bigger audiences, which brought bigger revenue, which brought higher salaries for all players."[26]

Despite the draft, however, the Bears and Giants continued their winning ways. Chicago, in particular, continued to come up with one talented player after another.

Sid Luckman, Bill Osmanski, Ken Kavanagh, and Bulldog Turner made certain the Bears—known as the "Monsters of the Midway"—were always in contention. The best example of Chicago's dominance was their record-setting 73-0 win over the Redskins in the 1940 title game, the first radio network broadcast of an NFL contest. It would not be until after World War II that another club—the Cleveland Browns—would dominate the league.

CHAPTER 4

A National Obsession

THE NATIONAL FOOTBALL League had come a long way since its birth in 1920, but still had far to go to approach the popularity of the college game. A hint of the possibilities that the new medium of television presented were seen with the first broadcast of an NFL game on October 22, 1939. The onset of World War II, however, interrupted the league's progress in becoming a major sports institution.

The War Years

Many colleges lost star players to the military during World War II. Programs not affected were those of the service academies. The United States Military Academy at West Point was the dominant team of the period. The Army squads of 1944, 1945, and 1946 were led by perhaps the greatest one-two punch in college history, fullback Doc Blanchard and halfback Glenn Davis.

The undefeated 1946 Army team huddles during a practice.

From 1944 to 1946, "Mr. Inside" and "Mr. Outside," as they were known, led the Cadets to three undefeated seasons (with one tie in 1946) and two national championships. They are the only two running backs from the same school to win the Heisman Trophy in successive seasons, doing so in 1945 and 1946, respectively.

National Football League teams were also decimated as players, coaches, and front office personnel were called off to fight. All told, some 638 active NFL players served in the war and twenty-one lost their lives. For a time, the league considered suspending operations. As newly appointed commissioner Elmer Layden explained, however, "we're going ahead and planning for conduct of our regular schedule. But everything we decide today may have to be abandoned tomorrow. While we believe professional football has a definite place in the recreational program of a nation at war, nothing connected with it should or will be permitted to hinder the war effort."[27]

The league continued play while making several noteworthy adjustments. In 1943, the Cleveland Rams received permission to halt operations for a year because co-owner Dan Reeves was in the Navy, thus reducing the league to nine clubs. The number shrank to eight when the Pittsburgh Steelers and Philadelphia Eagles merged forces, calling themselves the Steagles. The next year, the Boston Yanks were awarded a franchise. The Eagles once again began to operate on their own, and the Steelers merged with the Chicago Cardinals to form Card-Pitt. The "Carpets," as they were referred to, lost all ten of their games and many consider them to be the worst team of all time.

Still, the league managed to survive the war years and optimistically looked to the future. The postwar economy was booming and fans turned out to see the returning players. Sammy Baugh of the Washington Redskins established himself as the first of the modern quarterbacks, showing just how vital a passing quarterback could be to a team's offense. Most teams now employed the T-formation, which changed the game's focus from power to speed and deception. As Halas described it, "Football became a game of brains."[28]

With interest in the pro game on the upswing, it was not surprising that investors began to think of the sport as a way to make money. The NFL soon found itself with competition.

The All-America Football Conference

Chicago Tribune sports editor Arch Ward had been the organizer of the first baseball all-star game and football's Chicago All-Star Game. In August 1945, he announced the formation of the All-America Football Conference (AAFC). In addition to its familiarity as a popular sports term, the All-America name was selected to indicate the league's scope, spanning, as it did, the entire country. The new association included the Brooklyn

Washington Redskins quarterback Sammy Baugh (left), the first of the game's modern quarterbacks.

Dodgers, Buffalo Bisons, Miami Seahawks, and New York Yankees in the Eastern Division and the Chicago Rockets, Cleveland Browns, Los Angeles Dons, and San Francisco 49ers in the Western Division. Because of the far-ranging distances between these cities, the league became, by necessity, the first pro football league to travel by air.

Jim Crowley, one of Notre Dame's famous "Four Horsemen," was named the league's commissioner. Securing players was not a problem. Between returning servicemen and graduating college stars, there was plenty of talent to go around. "There were enough players available to stock a dozen leagues,"[29] remarked Crowley. The AAFC signed forty of the sixty-six College All-Stars, and 100 former NFL players.

Some of the league's more recognizable names included Elroy "Crazylegs" Hirsch, Angelo Bertelli, Frank Sinkwich, Frankie Albert, and Otto Graham. The AAFC had attempted to reach an agreement with the NFL to respect each other's player contracts (not try to sign players belonging to teams in the other league), and arrange a possible season-ending "world series." The more established league, however, could not be bothered by the upstarts. "Let them get a football and play a game," snorted commissioner Layden, "and then maybe we'll have something to talk about."[30]

The product the AAFC put on the field was well received by the fans. With its teams using several of the country's largest stadiums, the league actually averaged more fans

INTEGRATION

Professional football had been integrated as far back as 1904, when Charles W. Follis starred for the Shelby, Ohio, team. Fritz Pollard and Bobby Marshall integrated the American Professional Football Association in 1920, and the occasional black player could be found on NFL rosters until 1934. The failure of any to appear after that was likely a result of owners' fears of alienating white fans by giving jobs to blacks during the Depression. In 1946, the Los Angeles Rams signed tailback Kenny Washington and end Woody Strode. Rather than intentionally trying to strike a blow for equality, the Rams inked the pair after being informed they could not lease the Los Angeles Coliseum unless they agreed to allow local hero Washington to try out. Strode was signed, in part, to give Washington a teammate with whom to room. In the All-America Football Conference, Cleveland broke the color line by signing guard Bill Willis and fullback Marion Motley. Both players were elected to the Pro Football Hall of Fame when their playing days were

Woody Strode (far left) and Kenny Washington (far right) broke the NFL's color barrier in 1946.

over. Several years would pass, however, until blacks began appearing on league rosters in appreciable numbers.

per game than did the older, more established NFL. In the AAFC's very first game, the Cleveland Browns defeated the Miami Seahawks in front of 60,135 fans, the largest crowd ever to witness a regular-season professional football game. The Browns, coached by Paul Brown, proved to be the powerhouse of the league. They finished with the best regular-season record—and won the

championship—in each of the AAFC's four seasons in existence.

Competition between the leagues, however, led to the All-America Football Conference's eventual downfall. Teams from both circuits competed for players, driving salaries to new heights. The lack of other teams as good as the Browns was also a likely contributing factor to the league's demise. A 30 percent drop in attendance in 1949 signaled that the end was near. That December, the two leagues agreed to merge, and the Browns, 49ers, and Colts joined the NFL to create a thirteen-team league divided into American and National conferences. In a special allocation draft, the thirteen clubs were able to choose players from the disbanded teams.

The established NFL teams considered the three new clubs to be inferior. Washington Redskins owner George Preston Marshall bragged, "The worst team in our league could beat the best team in theirs."[31] All expected the NFL-champion Philadelphia Eagles to defeat the AAFC-champion Cleveland

Cleveland Browns quarterback Otto Graham holds his Most Valuable Player trophy with coach Paul Brown.

Browns easily when the two met in the new club's first regular-season contest. The Browns, however, had different plans. With more than 71,000 fans in the stands, Cleveland routed Philadelphia by a score of 35-10. They proceeded to ride roughshod over the rest of the league on their way to the American Conference crown. The Browns then defeated the Los Angeles Rams, 30-28, to win their first National Football League title.

The Television Game

In addition to the merging of the leagues, the year 1950 brought other noteworthy changes. The NFL had been experimenting with a rule allowing unlimited substitutions of players. Its final adoption in 1950 put an end to the age of the two-way player. From this point on, teams employed separate teams on offense and defense, with specialists for jobs such as punting and placekicking. The onset of the two-platoon game raised the skill level required of the players. Efforts could now be concentrated on excelling at one position, rather than at two.

Also in 1950, the game emerged as a television sport. As early as 1947, the Bears had tried to muster interest in the game through the new medium. In exchange for a fee of $4,500, George Halas allowed station WBKB to televise all six of the team's home games. His experiment proved successful, as both attendance and revenue rose. As the number of television sets increased, however, Halas became less generous, allowing only one game to be broadcast the following year. He feared more and more people would prefer to watch the games free, at home, which would eventually bring about a decline in attendance.

For 1950, the Los Angeles Rams (recently transplanted from Cleveland) agreed to allow all their games, both home and

THE FIRST NFL SCANDAL

Shortly before the New York Giants were to meet the Chicago Bears to decide the NFL championship on December 15, 1946, recently appointed commissioner Bert Bell faced a difficult decision. New York fullback Merle Hapes and tailback Frankie Filchock reportedly had been offered $2,500 each to see to it that the Bears covered the ten-point spread. Although the bribes were not accepted, neither player reported the offer. Bell forbade Hapes from playing in the contest, but not Filchock, since the tailback denied ever being propositioned. Filchock suffered a broken nose early in the game, but threw two touchdown passes in the Giants' 24-14 loss.

Eventually it was learned that a twenty-eight-year-old gambler by the name of Alvin J. Paris had made the bribe attempts. He was convicted on two counts of bribery, and served nine months in jail. The New York Times called the incident "the biggest sports scandal since the 1919 World Series."

At the trial, Filchock admitted that he had lied about receiving the offer. Although Bell announced that the two players would be suspended indefinitely, Filchock was reinstated in 1950 and Hapes four years later.

away, to be televised. The team's attendance fell, but the benefits of television became obvious as more and more people became exposed to the product. The next year, the team aired only its road games, and attendance once again shot up. The Redskins followed the Rams on the air, with other teams doing the same in short order.

The first network telecasts of games took place in 1951. The Dumont Network broadcast five regular-season contests, as well as the championship game between the Rams and Browns. The network continued to blaze the way until it folded in 1955. By that time, the league had come to agreement on a broadcasting policy, which the courts supported. Broadcasts of games were prohibited in the home team's city; away games, that did not affect attendance, would still be aired.

Broadcasting policies did not hinder the way the game was played, however, and the Browns continued their dominance through the first half of the '50s. They made it to the championship game in each of the next five seasons, winning in 1954 and 1955. The Giants replaced them as champs in 1956, but rookie running sensation Jim Brown led Cleveland back to the title game once more the next year.

In 1957, the Baltimore Colts stepped forward. The original Colts franchise, which had come over from the AAFC, folded after compiling a 1-11 record in 1951. The city reentered the league in 1953 when it was awarded the franchise abandoned by the defunct Dallas Texans. Led by quarterback Johnny Unitas, the club compiled the first winning record in its history in 1957. Its finest moment, however, was still to come.

The Greatest Game Ever Played

Many people consider December 28, 1958, as the date the National Football League came into its own. That day, the Baltimore Colts met the New York Giants for the league championship before more than 64,000 fans in Yankee Stadium in New York.

Legendary Baltimore Colts quarterback Johnny Unitas led his team to its first winning record in 1957.

In addition to Unitas, whom many consider the greatest quarterback ever, the Colts' offensive weapons included running backs Lenny Moore and Alan Ameche and receiver Raymond Berry. Charlie Conerly, Frank Gifford, and Kyle Rote were key figures in the New York attack. Both clubs had strong defenses.

The game was one of the first championship contests to be televised nationally (it was blacked out in the New York area). More than three-quarters of all American families had television sets by 1958. Those who saw the game will never forget it.

Baltimore capitalized on two New York fumbles to take a 14-3 lead at the half. The Giants bounced back with two scores of their own to pull ahead, 17-14. With two minutes to go in the game, New York had a chance to seal the victory when fate intervened. Needing four yards, New York's Frank Gifford ran for what appeared to be a first down. However, Baltimore defensive end Gino Marchetti had his leg broken on the play. Before spotting the ball, the referee waited until a stretcher was called for and Marchetti was carried off the field. In the confusion, claimed the Giants, he misspotted it. "He was too concerned about Marchetti," said Kyle Rote. "I saw him pick it up at his front foot and put it down where his back foot was."[32] The ball was placed just shy of the first down, and the Giants were forced to punt.

The New York Giants score a touchdown against the Baltimore Colts during the famous 1958 NFL championship game.

Starting at their own fourteen-yard line with less than two minutes to go in the game, Unitas drove the Colts the length of the field as time was running down. With only seven seconds left in regulation time, Steve Myhra kicked a twenty-yard field goal to tie the game. The contest went into overtime, the first NFL Championship Game to ever do so.

The Giants won the toss and chose to receive to begin the overtime period. Baltimore held them, however, and New York was forced to punt. The Colts got possession on their own twenty, and Unitas proceeded once again to lead them down the field. At eight minutes and fifteen seconds into overtime, Unitas handed off to fullback Alan Ameche who plowed into the end zone from one yard out for the winning touchdown and the championship.

The effect of the game, which became known as "The Greatest Game Ever Played," cannot be underestimated. ABC Sports executive Dennis Lewin later said, "I think the NFL as a national entity first came alive on television with the Giants-Colts championship game in 1958. That exposure on a national level, with one of the greatest games ever played, launched pro football into the American consciousness."[33] Nearly eleven million homes across America were tuned to the game. The National Football League had finally arrived.

The League Faces Another Challenge

The increasing interest in the sport was not lost on Texas millionaire Lamar Hunt. In

1958 Hunt had tried, unsuccessfully, to buy the Chicago Cardinals and move them to Dallas. Spurned by the NFL, he decided to form his own league. Together with fellow Texan Bud Adams, Hunt established a new eight-team league—the American Football League—with franchises in Boston, Buffalo, Dallas, Denver, Houston, Los Angeles, New York, and Oakland. Former South Dakota governor Joe Foss was named the league's first commissioner.

To attract attention, the new league instituted some minor changes. After scoring a touchdown, a team had the option of kicking the extra point or trying for a two-point conversion by running or throwing the ball into the end zone. To help the fans get to know the players better, names were put on the back of the uniforms.

Realizing that offense attracts fans, AFL teams went after the best quarterbacks available, building their offenses around the pass. Veterans such as George Blanda, Frank Tripucka, and Babe Parilli won jobs directing teams in the new league. Another significant addition was halfback Billy Cannon, winner of the Heisman Trophy, who signed with the Houston Oilers. With Blanda throwing and Cannon running, the Oilers made it to the AFL championship game in 1960, where they defeated the Los

Angeles Chargers, 14-10, to become the league's first champions.

In the NFL, thirty-three-year-old Pete Rozelle was installed as the league's new commissioner in 1960 following the death of Bert Bell. A former general manager of the Los Angeles Rams, Rozelle was an expert in marketing and public relations. By the time he retired in 1989, he would be recognized, arguably, as the most successful commissioner in pro sports history.

Rozelle convinced the owners it would benefit them to join together to negotiate a network television contract, rather than to distribute games locally to affiliates. In 1964 a two-year deal was signed with CBS

Pete Rozelle was the commissioner of the NFL from 1960 to 1989.

under which each team received $1 million per year. (The AFL signed a five-year deal with NBC that same year.)

By this time, the two leagues were in an all-out battle to sign the top graduating college stars. Salaries increased at a rapid rate, with six-figure bonuses making them even more attractive. Although the NFL signed most of the big-name stars, the AFL scored an important victory in 1965 when the New York Jets inked Alabama quarterback Joe Namath to a contract for a record $437,000. The brash, talented, good-looking Namath was just what the new league needed. "Broadway Joe," so-called because of his love of the night life in the media capital of the country, became the league's best-known player.

The NFL countered with quarterbacks such as Fran Tarkenton, Sonny Jurgensen, and John Brodie. The most successful team of the decade was the run-oriented Green Bay Packers led by coach Vince Lombardi. Lombardi preached a strict, disciplined approach while guiding the Pack to NFL titles in 1961 and 1962. Bart Starr directed Green Bay's attack, which focused on careful execution and the running of fullback Jim Taylor and halfback Paul Hornung. "I demand a commitment to excellence and to victory," explained Lombardi, "and that is what life is all about."[34]

THE MYSTERIOUS NELSON ROSS

Until about forty years ago, quarterback John K. Brallier was believed to have been the first professional football player. The nineteen-year-old Brallier freely admitted to having received $10 per game, plus expenses, from the Latrobe (Pa.) YMCA team in 1895.

Around 1962, however, a man walked into the offices of Daniel M. Rooney of the Pittsburgh Steelers. He handed Rooney a paper he had researched on the early days of pro football in the state. After a brief visit, the stranger left and Rooney began to read the report. The more he read, the more intrigued he became. Unfortunately, the paper was unsigned and Rooney was not certain of the man's name, although he believed it to be Nelson Ross. Rooney enlisted the aid of the Pittsburgh newspapers to locate the gentleman, but without success. When the Pro Football Hall of Fame was constructed in 1963, Rooney donated the paper.

According to the *NFL's Official Encyclopedic History of Professional Football*, along with the report was a yellowing piece of paper headed, "Expense Accounting Allegheny Athletic Assoc. Football Club." The sheet had been prepared by O. D. Thompson, the manager of the club, in 1892. In the middle of the page was a listing for the game of November 12, 1892, versus the Pittsburg A.C. One of the entries read, "game performance bonus to W. Heffelfinger for playing (cash) $500.00."

Through the examination of old newspaper accounts, Ross' findings were later confirmed by Thomas Jable, another researcher, and Dick McCann of the Pro Football Hall of Fame. These are the earliest records in existence proving payment to an individual for playing football.

In April 1966, Foss resigned as AFL commissioner. He was replaced by Oakland Raiders coach, Al Davis. Shortly afterward, the Giants of the rival league signed Buffalo Bills kicker Pete Gogolak, who had played out his option. In retaliation, Davis indicated that the AFL would try to sign certain NFL stars. This threat of an escalation in the bidding war for players was just the incentive the leagues needed to reach an accord.

In a surprise proclamation on June 8, NFL commissioner Rozelle announced that the two leagues had agreed to merge. Outrageous bonus payments for players would end, and a common college draft was set to take place beginning in 1967. The leagues would not have interleague play until the 1970 season, when their current television contracts expired. At that time, three NFL teams—the Browns, Colts, and Steelers—would join the ten AFL teams to form the American Football Conference. The remaining NFL teams would constitute the National Football Conference. The champions of the leagues would then meet in a title contest. No one had any idea that the championship game would eventually become the Super Bowl, the single biggest one-day sports event in the country.

Equality

Until the leagues merged, however, the champions of the two leagues would meet in the AFL-NFL World Championship

Green Bay Packers players carry Vince Lombardi off the field after a Super Bowl win in 1968.

Game. (It would not officially become the Super Bowl until game III in 1969.) The first contest took place on January 15, 1967. The Green Bay Packers of the NFL met the Kansas City Chiefs of the AFL in the Los Angeles Memorial Coliseum in California. As they did when the Browns entered the league in 1950, NFL owners looked forward to seeing the Packers demolish the team from the upstart league. Unlike 1950, they were not disappointed.

Playing a surprisingly competitive Chiefs club, the Packers moved out to a 14-10 halftime lead. The second half, however, was all Green Bay. The Packers scored three more touchdowns while holding Kansas City scoreless, giving them a 35-10 victory.

The next year, Green Bay followed a similar script. This time playing Al Davis' Oakland Raiders, Lombardi's troops took a 16-7 lead into the locker room at halftime, then finished the job in the second half, coming out on top by a score of 33-14. This second consecutive victory in the World Championship Game gave ammunition to the many football observers who maintained that the new teams did not measure up to the best the older league had to offer. Lombardi probably added to this feeling by remarking that the victory "wasn't our best."[35]

Shortly after the game, Lombardi announced his retirement as the Packers head coach. Green Bay dropped to third place in the Central Division in 1968, opening the door for the Baltimore Colts, who took the NFL crown. Their opponents in Super Bowl III were none other than Joe Namath's New York Jets. Virtually no one gave the New Yorkers much of a chance in the contest, as the oddsmakers made the powerful Colts an eighteen-point favorite. No one, that is, except Broadway Joe. On the Thursday prior to the game, while accepting a Miami Touchdown Club award as pro football's outstanding player, Namath shocked those in the audience when he said, "We're going to win Sunday. I'll guarantee you."[36]

Sunday came, and Namath backed up his words. He completed 17 of 28 passes for 206 yards while fullback Matt Snell rushed for 121. The Jets opened up a 16-0 lead before surrendering a meaningless touchdown in the fourth quarter. The final score of 16-7 was not as close as it seemed. With the victory, the American Football League finally was accorded the respect it deserved. No longer could it be considered the NFL's inferior.

After the Merger

Professional football in the 1960s was certainly the most wide-open version of the game the sport had ever seen. Accurate passing and exciting running made the offensive game even more attractive to fans. Improvements on offense stimulated improvements on the other side of the line. Defenses, such as those of the Detroit Lions and the Los Angeles Rams, became known for their ferocious front four linemen. Blitzing linebackers made headlines, and the quarterback sack became a new statistic.

During the 1970s, a media phenomenon occurred that played a large part in establishing football as the spectator sport of choice. *Monday Night Football* became part of the nation's consciousness. Movie attendance and crime declined on Mondays, as more and more people stayed home to watch broadcasters Howard Cosell, Frank Gifford, and Don Meredith entertain and inform. To many, the game became almost secondary.

The teams which dominated the 1970s were four former league doormats: the Dallas Cowboys, Miami Dolphins, Minnesota

Vikings, and Pittsburgh Steelers. Dallas teams featured the quarterback skills of Roger Staubach, the running of Calvin Hill and Tony Dorsett, and the receiving of Preston Pearson and Drew Pearson. Bob Lilly and Randy White anchored the defense as the Cowboys made four appearances in the Super Bowl, winning in 1972 and 1978.

The Dolphins were coached by NFL career-wins leader Don Shula. His offense centered around quarterback Bob Griese and running backs Jim Kiick, Larry Csonka, and Mercury Morris. Miami's "No Name Defense," sparked by linebacker Nick Buoniconti, always kept them in the game. After reaching the Super Bowl for the first time in 1971, the Dolphins won it all the next year, becoming the only team in history to go an entire season without losing

a game. Miami also won Super Bowl VIII the following season.

Scrambling quarterback Fran Tarkenton led Bud Grant's Minnesota club, with Chuck Foreman eating up yards on the ground. The Vikings' defense was led by their remarkable front line, known as the "Purple People Eaters." Defensive tackle Alan Page headed the outfit, winning the league's Most Valuable Player award in 1971. The Vikings won six consecutive division titles between 1973 and 1978, but failed to take the Super Bowl in three attempts over that period.

The Steelers were the most successful of the four clubs, winning four Super Bowls over the course of six years (1974, 1975, 1978, 1979). Franco Harris' runs and Terry Bradshaw's tosses to Lynn Swann and John

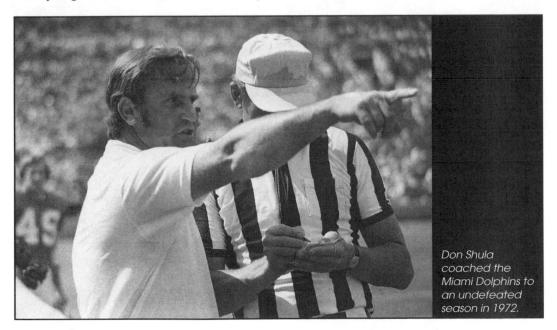

Don Shula coached the Miami Dolphins to an undefeated season in 1972.

Stallworth put points on the board. A defense led by "Mean" Joe Greene, Mel Blount, and Jack Lambert earned itself the nickname the "Steel Curtain."

Decades of Change

The success of the pros depended on the ability of the colleges to continue to provide them with talent. Colleges continued to turn out one star after another and became known for producing All-Americas at specific positions. The University of Southern California was a hotbed for fleet-footed running backs, with Anthony Davis, Ricky Bell, Charles White, and O. J. Simpson counted among its alumni. Quarterbacks were harvested from Brigham Young University (Jim McMahon, Steve Young, and

Ty Detmer) and the University of Miami (Jim Kelly, Bernie Kosar, Vinny Testaverde, and Steve Walsh). Coach Joe Paterno seemed to manufacture linebackers at Penn State, while power runners came down the assembly line at Ohio State.

Such a pipeline of talent assured the pro game of continued success. In the 1980s and 1990s, offenses became more sophisticated as a new generation of quarterbacks, led by Joe Montana, Dan Marino, and John Elway, made its mark on the game. Defenses scrambled to keep up. Teams switched to four-man linebacking alignments to contain larger and stronger runners and receivers.

The outstanding team of this period was clearly the San Francisco 49ers. With coach

Joe Montana and Jerry Rice (no. 80) formed the core of the San Francisco 49ers' potent offense.

Bill Walsh calling the shots (succeeded by George Seifert in 1989), quarterback Montana, fullback Roger Craig, end Jerry Rice, and a defense led by Ronnie Lott carried the 49ers to seven Western Division NFC titles in the 1980s. The team went to the Super Bowl four times—in 1981, 1984, 1988, and 1989—and came out on top each year. The Redskins and Raiders each won a pair of titles in the decade.

The 1990s found the Dallas Cowboys challenging the 49ers for league supremacy. Led by quarterback Troy Aikman, running back Emmitt Smith, and receiver Michael Irvin, the Cowboys won three Super Bowls in a four-year span (1993, 1994, 1996). San Francisco and Denver each took a pair of titles in the last decade of the century.

Significant changes were also occurring off the field of play. Owners relocated franchises in a search for more profitable markets. In 1980, Oakland owner Al Davis petitioned the league for permission to move his team to Los Angeles, but was denied. He took the league to court, suing for antitrust violations (those concerning business monopolies). Two years later, when the courts ruled in his favor, Davis made the move. He soon pressured Los Angeles for a new stadium. When he was turned down, he moved the team back to Oakland in 1995.

In 1984, the Baltimore Colts relocated to Indianapolis. The Browns eventually transferred to Baltimore in 1996, becoming the Ravens, while Cleveland got a new club

ARENA FOOTBALL

On February 11, 1981, former National Football League Properties executive James F. Foster was watching an indoor soccer game at Madison Square Garden in New York. During the contest, it occurred to him that football could also be adapted to indoor play. He began scribbling a sketch of a miniature football field on a manila envelope, together with suggestions of how to modify the game. Changes would include using a fifty-yard field, eight players on each side, and rebound nets along the sidelines. Knowing the sport could not compete with the established NFL, Foster speculated on a summer alternative.

Around the same time, however, the United States Football League was proposed as a summer league. Foster shelved his idea until 1985, after the USFL had proved a failure. To get an idea of public response to his brainchild, he arranged a test game to be played in Rockford, Illinois, in April 1986. Positive reaction led to a "showcase game" on February 26 of the following year. The Arena Football League debuted that June.

The league began its first season in 1987 with four teams: the Chicago Bruisers, Denver Dynamite, Pittsburgh Gladiators, and Washington Commandos. Denver defeated Pittsburgh in Arena Bowl I to become the first league champion. An average of more than 11,000 fans per game enjoyed the league's wide-open, high-scoring style of play.

With the year 2000, the league begins its fourteenth season of play. Several of its players have gone on to play in the NFL, including the star of Super Bowl XXXIV, St. Louis Rams quarterback Kurt Warner.

two years later, retaining the name Browns. The Los Angeles Rams and Houston Oilers also moved before the year 2000, shifting to St. Louis (which had lost the Cardinals to Phoenix) and Tennessee (where they are now known as the Titans), respectively.

As new markets opened, team revenues increased. Players sought to increase their salaries and labor unrest became a major issue. In 1982, the players proposed a profit-sharing plan that would give them 55 percent of team revenues. The owners refused, and a fifty-seven-day-long strike followed. The owners held fast, but the players had made their point. Their plan would eventually lead to a salary-cap agreement in the 1990s, whereby the amount that a team could spend on player salaries was limited.

The players walked out again in 1987, with free agency as one of the key issues. Players wanted the opportunity to choose the team for which they wanted to play. This time, however, the owners decided to continue playing out the schedule with "replacement" players. After twenty-four days, the regular players returned to action. The owners and NFL Players Association came to agreement on a form of limited free agency. A total of 229 players took advantage of this opportunity and changed teams, usually for much higher salaries.

With teams and players in such a state of transition, it is, perhaps, surprising that the league continues to thrive. Such has been the case, with new stars carrying on the traditions of those who came before. Players like Brett Favre, Marshall Faulk, and Terrell Davis proved themselves worthy successors, with others like Peyton Manning, Randy Moss, and Keyshawn Johnson hot on their heels. The future seems bright, indeed, for America's favorite sport.

CHAPTER 5

The Greats of the Game

P ART OF FOOTBALL'S appeal lies in its larger-than-life stars. Youngsters grow up dreaming of becoming the next John Elway, Barry Sanders, or Jerry Rice. They fantasize about winning the Super Bowl with a clutch pass, a dazzling run, or a one-handed grab in the end zone, or of performing feats that will someday land them in the Football Hall of Fame among the galaxy of stars who are part of football's enduring legacy.

Joe Montana

The Joe Montana legend began at the University of Notre Dame in 1975. With the Fighting Irish losing 30-10 in the fourth quarter of a game against Air Force, Montana guided his team to three touchdowns in eight minutes for a miraculous 31-30 victory.

In the pros, Montana established a reputation as perhaps the greatest clutch performer in NFL history. Remarked former 49ers coach Bill Walsh, "When the game is on the line, and you need someone to go in there and win it right now, I would rather have Joe Montana as my quarterback than anyone who ever played the game."[37] Montana was at his best when the stakes were highest. He directed thirty-one winning fourth-quarter comebacks, including one to win Super Bowl XXIII. He led the San Francisco 49ers to four Super Bowl wins and was named the game's Most Valuable Player on three occasions.

At his retirement, Montana was the all-time NFL leader in passing accuracy, having completed better than 63 percent of all his throws. He completed more than 60 percent of his passes in eight consecutive seasons, and recorded a high of 70.2 percent in 1989. No one has ever compiled a lower interception rate for a career than Montana's 2.58 per hundred passes. His consistent high level of performance will be hard to duplicate.

Dan Marino

The numbers posted by Dan Marino in his seventeen NFL seasons with the Miami

Miami Dolphins quarterback Dan Marino shattered many passing records.

Dolphins may never be duplicated. A product of the quarterback hotbed of western Pennsylvania, Marino completed 4,967 passes in his career, 420 of which were caught for touchdowns. No other quarterback has thrown for even 350 scores. Marino passed for an incredible 61,361 yards (nearly 35 miles), almost 10,000 yards more than his nearest challenger.

No one was more of a competitor than Marino, nor more respected by his opponents. As Buffalo Bills all-pro defensive end Bruce Smith explained, "Playing him, it wasn't just his talent that stood out. There was a professionalism, a respect you didn't see very much with other guys."[38]

Marino was an emotional leader whose unerring throws hit their intended targets with laser-like accuracy. His exceptionally quick release allowed him to wait until the last second before throwing the ball, giving his receivers a chance to break free. It also helped him avoid being sacked as often as other quarterbacks.

Still, NFL teams cannot reach the league's upper echelon of clubs without having a balanced attack. Because Miami's running game never approached the level of its passing game, Marino never won a Super Bowl championship.

ERNIE NEVERS' 40-POINT GAME

Ernie Nevers was one of the greatest athletes Stanford University ever produced. He won eleven varsity letters for the Cardinals, starring in baseball, basketball, and football. After graduation, he played all three sports professionally.

His greatest success came on the football field. In 1950, the Associated Press named him the fourth-best college player of the half century behind Jim Thorpe, Red Grange, and Bronko Nagurski.

On Thanksgiving Day, November 28, 1929, Nevers put on a performance for the Chicago Cardinals that was worthy of the record books. As the Cardinals player/coach, he scored six touchdowns that day against the Chicago Bears, and kicked 4 extra points, for a total of 40 points. Nevers scored all of the Cardinals' points in the 40-6 victory, setting a professional scoring mark that has lasted seventy years. The Bears did not allow 40 points in any other game that season.

Sammy Baugh

Sid Luckman had no doubts at all about who was football's greatest player. "Sammy Baugh was the best player ever," reminisced the Hall of Fame quarterback. "Nobody is ever going to equal him. Not anybody."[39] Those who saw Baugh perform for the Washington Redskins in 1943 would likely agree with Luckman. "Slingin' Sammy" led the NFL in passing that year, throwing for 1,754 yards and 23 touchdowns. On defense, he led the league with 11 interceptions from the defensive back position. To top it all, he also led the NFL in punting, notching an average of 45.9 yards per punt. No player has ever led the league in such a wide variety of categories.

Baugh played sixteen seasons with the Redskins, and rewrote the record books. He led the NFL in passing six times and in punting for four consecutive years. At the time of his retirement, he held the career records for most passes, completions, touchdown passes, and completion percentage. Several of his marks, including those for highest punting average in a season and career, are still standing nearly half a century after his retirement from the game.

Considering his record, it is amazing to think that Baugh did not play quarterback for Washington until his fifth season in the league. He began his career as a tailback and also played safety on defense. He once intercepted four passes in a game to break a league mark.

Baugh revolutionized the game with his passing. He threw the ball on any down, at any time, in an age when most coaches considered it a last resort. Baugh's accuracy was legendary. When he first reported to the Redskins as a rookie, coach Ray Flaherty reportedly told him, "On this one, I want you to hit the receiver in the eye."

"One question," replied the confident newcomer. "Which eye?"[40]

Jim Brown

At Syracuse University, Jim Brown was much more than just an All-America football player. He also made All-American in lacrosse, lettered in basketball, and when a sophomore, placed fifth in the national decathlon championship. On the gridiron, he set a major college record in his senior year when he scored forty-three points against Colgate (6 touchdowns, 7 PATs).

Brown was the fifth player selected in the 1957 NFL draft, joining coach Paul Brown on the Cleveland Browns. His nine seasons with Cleveland cemented his standing as the ultimate fullback. He had the power to run over people and the speed to run around them. Brown led the league in rushing eight times, gaining a career total of 12,312 yards on the ground. In 1966, at the age of thirty, he retired to pursue a career in movies.

Upon his retirement, he held the records for most touchdowns scored in a season (21) and in a career (126). He ran for 100 or more yards in a game on fifty-eight occasions and for 200 or more four times. His most incredible mark of all may have been that, in nine seasons, he never missed a single down because of injury, despite being the focal point of the Browns' attack and the target of every opposing defense. In response to charges that he overused his star runner, Paul Brown ex-

Fullback Jim Brown could outrun and overpower defenses.

plained, "When you've got the biggest cannon, you shoot it."[41]

Walter Payton

There have been more punishing NFL runners than Chicago's Walter Payton. There have also been faster, shiftier runners, and those who were better blockers. There have never been any, however, who combined these talents, together with an outstanding work ethic, in one complete package. "Without a doubt," said his former coach, Mike Ditka, "Walter is the most complete football player I've ever seen."[42]

Payton's rushing accomplishments include an all-time NFL career mark of 16,726 yards (including 10 seasons of 1,000 or more), 77 games with 100 or more yards, and a high of 275 yards in a 1977 contest against the Vikings. He was also a threat as a receiver, catching 492 passes out of the backfield.

Payton never gave less than his best, playing every game as if it were his last. Despite his relatively small size (five foot, ten inches, 202 pounds), he was extremely durable. In thirteen NFL seasons, all with the Bears, Payton missed only one game. He carried the ball 3,838 times in his career, more than any other back. Payton once said, "I'd like to be remembered as a guy . . . who stands for hard work and total effort."[43] No one will ever dispute the fact that he fulfilled that legacy.

Red Grange

It is hard to believe that anyone might have seen more football games than Amos Alonzo Stagg, who lived to the age of 102, and coached college football for fifty-seven years. In his estimation, Red Grange's performance against Michigan in 1924 was "the most spectacular single-handed performance ever delivered in a major game."[44]

Grange, a running back for Illinois, began by returning the opening kickoff ninety-five yards for a touchdown. The next time he touched the ball, he raced sixty-seven yards for a second score. His third carry resulted in a fifty-six-yard touchdown run. A fourth TD came on a forty-four-yard reverse on his sixth carry of the game. Grange gained a total of 265 yards, and scored four touchdowns, in the first twelve minutes of play,

Chicago Bears running back Walter Payton, one of the game's most durable ball carriers.

giving Illinois a 27-0 lead. He sat out the rest of the half, then returned with a thirteen-yard run for a fifth score in the third period. In the fourth quarter, he threw a pass to teammate Marion Leonard for yet another touchdown. He finished the contest with an incredible 402 total yards. It was at this game that the legendary sportswriter Grant-

land Rice allegedly dubbed Grange the "Galloping Ghost."

Grange was a three-time All-American for the Illini. Following his graduation, he signed with the Chicago Bears in the NFL's infancy. His contract called for a then un-heard of $100,000, plus a percentage of the gate. With Grange as their drawing card, the

THE DIRTIEST PLAYER EVER?

Football has always been a violent game and has had its share of mean players. Some of these toughs did not hesitate to do whatever was necessary to prevent an opponent from going about his job.

Former Chicago Bears defensive end Ed Sprinkle, for example, was the subject of a 1950 article in *Colliers* entitled, "The Meanest Man in Pro Football." He was known for throwing forearms and elbows at anything that moved. He once broke teammate Clyde "Bulldog" Turner's nose during a game with one of his misdirected blows.

San Francisco 49ers linebacker Hardy "The Hatchet" Brown was another player to fall in this category. He earned his reputation by throwing his shoulder under the chin of opposing players. In 1951, he was credited with knocking twenty-one players out of games, including the entire Washington Redskins backfield in one memorable contest.

Perhaps the dirtiest player of all was Conrad Dobler, a guard who played for the Cardinals, Bills, and Saints. Dobler enjoyed the notoriety he received for biting fingers, gouging eyes, and grabbing face masks. An example of his viciousness was his 1974 attack on Dallas Cowboys defensive back Cliff Harris, who was slowly getting up after being hurt from a block. In *The Football Hall of*

Guard Conrad Dobler was notorious for his dirty play.

Shame by Bruce Nash and Allan Zullo, Dobler described what happened: "I was about twenty yards away. But I thought, 'Why not?' . . . I hit him alongside the earlobe and his head bounced three or four times." Harris had to be taken off the field on a stretcher.

barnstorming Bears played an incredible nineteen games in sixty-six days. They broke attendance records wherever they played and helped establish pro football's legitimacy.

Bronko Nagurski

In seven seasons of his nine-year NFL career with the Chicago Bears, Bronislaw "Bronko" Nagurski rushed for a total of only 2,778 yards (no records are available for his first two seasons). He averaged fewer than ten carries per game and reached the 100-yard mark in a contest only once. By today's standards, those numbers are no better than average.

Nagurski, however, was anything but average. He was the first of the power backs, the biggest and most brutal runner of his day. His style was simple and direct. "Just before they got to me," he explained, "I'd put my shoulder down and ram 'em in the stomach. I'd knock 'em out of the way and keep running."[45] Nagurski was also a surprisingly good option passer. On defense, he played on the line and at linebacker. Rather than running him too often, Bears head coach George Halas used Nagurski in other ways. The six-foot, three-inch, 230-pound native of Rainy River, Ontario, Canada, was a ferocious blocker. When rookie running back Beattie Feathers joined Chicago in 1934, Nagurski often opened holes for him. He did this so well that Feath-

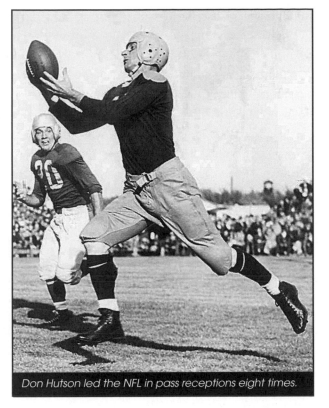

Don Hutson led the NFL in pass receptions eight times.

ers rushed for 1,004 yards, becoming the first NFL player in history to surpass the thousand-yard barrier. Nagurski was elected unanimously as a member of the first class inducted into the Pro Football Hall of Fame in 1963.

Don Hutson

An examination of Don Hutson's accomplishments as a member of the Green Bay Packers shows why he is generally considered to be the greatest wide receiver in history. In eleven NFL seasons, he led the league in touchdown catches nine times, in pass receptions eight times, in receiving yardage six times, and in scoring for five consecutive years. His seventy-four receptions in 1942 were forty-seven more than the number caught by anyone else (and more than that of four other entire teams). He was named to the all-pro squad nine times and was the Most Valuable Player in the league in both 1941 and 1942.

Before Hutson arrived on the scene, the forward pass played a minor role in NFL offenses. He is credited with having invented the first pass patterns ever run. His intelligence, speed, leaping ability, and sure hands enabled him to redefine his position. He broke most of the league records for receptions within his first five years as a pro. By the time he retired, he held nineteen marks in all.

Hutson's talents were not limited to catching the ball. He was an excellent placekicker, and played left end and right halfback on defense. Over his final six seasons in the league, he amassed a total of thirty interceptions.

Legendary coach George Allen put Hutson's career in perspective in no uncertain terms. "I don't think there's any doubt that Don Hutson was the greatest receiver ever," said Allen. "He improvised moves and devised patterns that have been copied ever since."[46]

Otto Graham

During his Hall of Fame career, Otto Graham did something that certainly will never

be matched. In all ten of his professional seasons, he led his team to the league championship game, winning on seven occasions. This is even more impressive considering that football was not even Graham's best sport. He attended Northwestern University on a basketball scholarship and eventually played pro ball with the Rochester Royals of the National Basketball League.

Graham was an All-American in both sports at Northwestern. Although he was a single-wing tailback in college, he was signed to be a T-formation quarterback by coach Paul Brown for his Cleveland football team of the upstart All-America Football Conference in 1946. As Brown explained, "Otto has the basic requirements of a T-quarterback—poise, ball handling, and distinct qualities of leadership."[47] Graham led the Browns to titles in each of the league's four seasons of existence.

When Cleveland joined the more established National Football League for the 1950 season, no one expected the team to continue its winning ways. In the club's first league game, however, Graham proved they were a force to be reckoned with. He led the Browns to a 35-10 trouncing of the defending champion Philadelphia Eagles. Cleveland went on to win the NFL title that season, with Graham throwing four touchdown passes in the championship game. The Browns lost to the Rams in 1951, and to the Lions in 1952 and 1953. Graham finished his career with titles in both 1954 and

1955, the latter after being coaxed out of retirement by coach Brown.

O. J. Simpson

It is certain that for years to come, people will argue over the guilt or innocence of O. J. Simpson in the murders of his wife, Nicole Brown Simpson, and her friend Ronald Goldman. Of what there can be no doubt is that Simpson was one of the greatest running backs who ever lived.

Simpson won the Heisman Trophy in 1968, capping a college career at the University of Southern California in which he led the nation in rushing in both 1967 and 1968. He was drafted by the Buffalo Bills but, amazingly, was used sparingly as a running back in his first three seasons in the league. "I think my best years have been wasted," he said. "When I came to the pros I was twenty-two years old, I could run the 100 in 9.4, and I was at my best athletically."[48]

When Lou Saban took over as coach in 1972, he turned O. J. loose. In Simpson's 1973 season, he became the first runner in the history of the National Football League to gain 2,000 yards in a season (2,003). Two years later, he rushed for more than 1,800 yards, caught 28 passes, and scored a then-record 23 touchdowns. For the five-year period from 1972 to 1976, Simpson carried the ball for 7,699 yards, or an average of nearly 110 per game. He rushed for 250 yards in a 1973 contest against New England to set a new single-game standard, then broke that mark three years later by carrying for 273 yards against Detroit.

Buffalo Bills running back O.J. Simpson, the first ball carrier to rush for 2,000 yards in one season.

Simpson retired as the second-leading rusher in NFL history, behind only Jim Brown. With all his records, however, he still missed out on every player's dream. In eleven NFL seasons, Simpson never played on a championship team.

Dick Butkus

Chicago Bears linebacker Dick Butkus was known as "Animal," and with good reason. There has never been a more ferocious player, with a greater drive to excel. "When they say all-pro middle linebacker," he said, "I want them to mean Butkus."[49]

Butkus was a first-round draft choice of the Bears in 1965 following an All-American career at the University of Illinois. It's hard to compare his record to that of more recent players at his position since sacks were not kept as an official statistic until the 1980s. He did average more than twelve tackles per game for his career, also collecting twenty-two interceptions and recovering twenty-three fumbles. He was a Pro Bowl selection every season from 1966 to 1973. In both 1969 and 1970, he was voted the NFL's Defensive Player of the Year.

The six-foot, three-inch, 245-pound Butkus suffered a knee injury in 1970 that limited his performance. That same year, NFL coaches were asked to name five players they would choose if they were putting together the ultimate team. Butkus received the most votes of any player. In 1979, he became the sixth linebacker inducted into the Pro Football Hall of Fame.

Lawrence Taylor

No one ever played the outside linebacker position quite like Lawrence Taylor. He had the strength to brush aside one blocker after another before stopping onrushing backs dead in their tracks, and could cover pass receivers with the best. He also had the speed and quickness to get around offensive linemen and run

Hall of Fame linebacker Dick Butkus averaged twelve tackles a game during his career.

THE GREATEST ATHLETE OF THEM ALL

No one knows for sure how Jim Thorpe would compare with any of the athletes of today. What is certain, however, is that he stood head and shoulders above those of the first half of the twentieth century. Thorpe played football under legendary coach Pop Warner at the Carlisle Indian School in Pennsylvania. His blazing speed and phenomenal power helped him to star on both offense and defense. Records from those days are sketchy at best, but in 1912, he is known to have scored 198 points for Carlisle, including twenty-five touchdowns. Thorpe later signed to play pro ball with the Canton Bulldogs and led them to three unofficial world championships, in 1916, 1917, and 1919.

Football, however, was hardly Thorpe's best sport. He excelled at every sport he tried, among them baseball, fencing, boxing, lacrosse, swimming, and wrestling. He became America's best-known athlete through his exploits in track and field. At the 1912 Olympics in Stockholm, Sweden, Thorpe won both the decathlon and pentathlon. As Peter King reported in his book, *Football: A History of the Professional Game*, during the medal ceremonies, King Gustav of Sweden told him, "Sir, you are the greatest athlete in the world." Thorpe was later stripped of his medals when it was learned he had played semipro baseball in 1909 and 1910. (They would eventually be returned to his descendants at a

Jim Thorpe was voted the greatest male athlete of the first half century in 1950.

ceremony during the 1984 Olympic Games in Los Angeles.)

Thorpe played pro football until 1928. He also played major league baseball for six seasons with the New York Giants, Cincinnati Reds, and Boston Braves. In 1950, the Associated Press voted him the greatest male athlete of the first half century.

down scrambling quarterbacks from behind. To do so many things well required an ability that can't be taught. "I can kind of read everything up and down the line," Taylor explained. "It's an instinct that tells me where to go. I don't know how that is, but it is."[50]

He played with a reckless abandon and love of the game that is seldom seen in modern players. Taylor's pride simply refused to allow him to be beaten by an opponent, whether in the Super Bowl or in a statistically meaningless exhibition game.

Taylor helped make the sack a glamorous statistic, finishing his career second on the all-time list with 132.5. He presented all kinds of challenges to opposing offenses. Said former Philadelphia Eagles head coach Dick Vermeil, "Taylor can cause you more problems in the preparation of an offensive game plan than any other single player I ever coached against."[51]

Anthony Muñoz

Deciding who is the best quarterback, running back, or linebacker is a tricky business, but at least there are numbers from which to make a comparison. Offensive linemen are entirely different. There are no completions, or rushing yards, or sacks to help tell the story. Many modern observers, however, feel that there has never been anyone better than Cincinnati Bengals tackle Anthony Muñoz.

Muñoz was drafted as the third overall pick in the 1980 NFL draft. He was considered a risky choice because of a knee injury that had plagued him at the University of Southern California. Nonetheless, the Bengals took the gamble and never regretted it.

His abilities helped raise him to near-legendary status among his contemporaries. At six-foot, six-inches tall and 285 pounds, Muñoz combined agility with exceptional strength. From his left tackle position, he could pull out on sweeps, block straight ahead on traps, and hold off defensive rushers on pass plays. As former team-mate Dave Lapham said, "I always laugh when I hear that somebody's going to be the next Michael Jordan or the next Anthony Muñoz. There's not going to be another."[52]

In thirteen seasons as a pro, Muñoz was elected to eleven consecutive Pro Bowls, was named All-Pro eleven straight times, and won NFL Offensive Lineman of the Year honors in 1981, 1987, and 1988. He helped Cincinnati grab three AFC Central Division titles and two AFC championships. In 1998, he became the first Hispanic player elected to the Pro Football Hall of Fame.

Paul Brown

Paul Brown was not the greatest offensive or defensive strategist of all time. He was, however, one of football's most successful coaches and one of its great innovators.

Brown was a successful high school and college coach in Ohio in the 1930s and 1940s. In the pros, he guided the Cleveland Browns (who were named for him) to ten consecutive championship games, four in the AAFC and six in the NFL. After leaving Cleveland, he became owner and coach of the expansion Cincinnati Bengals. Cincinnati made it to the Super Bowl twice under his management.

As an innovator, Brown had no peer. Among his many contributions to the game were the use of messenger guards to send plays in to the quarterback, spotters to fol-

Anthony Muñoz poses with his bust after becoming the first Hispanic player elected to the Pro Football Hall of Fame.

low the action on the field from high up in the stands, and intelligence and psychological tests to determine a player's ability to learn and improve. He was the first to establish full-time coaching staffs, scouting of college players, and training camps. He also brought playbooks and classroom instruction to the pro game.

Brown was a strict disciplinarian and a firm believer in the precise execution of fundamentals as the road to success. He strove for perfection and accepted nothing less from his players. His impact on the game was summed up by former San Francisco 49er coach Bill Walsh, one of his assistants in Cincinnati. Said Walsh, "Paul was . . . an innovator who bridged the gap from the '30s to the '90s. No one—not Halas or Lombardi or Rozelle—can make that claim in the history of pro football."[53]

Entering the Twenty-First Century

THE GAME OF football has evolved to a point far beyond what any of its founders could possibly have imagined. It has surpassed baseball as the nation's favorite sport, if the annual polls are to be believed, inciting passions at every level from high school through the pros. Today's players are faster, stronger, and bigger than those who played in years past. These superskilled athletes perform wondrous feats on the field and receive widespread media coverage for their heroics.

Though the college game retains millions of ardent supporters, the professional game has surged ahead in popularity. The days leading up to the Super Bowl have become a weeklong celebration, with all the attendant glamour and festivities making game day nothing less than a national holiday.

The professional game has been refined, with the latest tweaks working to the benefit of the offense. New rules instituted in the 1990s pushed kickoffs back to the 30-yard line (from the 35-yard line where they had been since 1974) and helped the passing game by limiting the amount of physical contact allowed between defensive backs and receivers. The two-point conversion was also adopted in 1994.

The next year, the Jacksonville Jaguars and Carolina Panthers entered the league. Both teams have already made the playoffs in their brief existence, underscoring the parity that has perhaps become inevitable as a result of the implementation of the salary cap. Every one of the league's thirty-one teams can dream of duplicating a turnaround like the one performed by the St. Louis Rams, who won Super Bowl XXXIV after finishing with a 4-12 record the previous season.

In recent years, the game has spread past national boundaries. In 1990, the National Football League scheduled several preseason games outside of the United States for the first time. A 1994 contest in Mexico City drew more than 112,000 fans. The reception

The St. Louis Rams went from a losing season to winning Super Bowl XXXIV the following year.

received by these games hinted at possible future league involvement on an international level. Today, the NFL Europe League has six teams—Amsterdam, Barcelona, Berlin, Frankfurt, Rhein, and Scotland— spreading football's gospel across the Continent.

Like every sport, however, football still has problems that must be addressed. Economic matters are always a concern as salaries continue to rapidly escalate. Network television has provided a major source of revenue for the NFL, with *Monday Night Football* being the sport's weekly showpiece since 1970. The future of the sport, however, might lie in pay-per-view showings, with free TV games decreasing in number.

As in every field of endeavor, racism occasionally surfaces in professional football. Minority representation still has far to go in the area of management positions. Progress is being made, but the feeling persists that African Americans and members of other minority groups simply do not receive the same consideration when coach and general manager openings arise. Many agree with Minnesota Vikings receiver Cris Carter when he says, "I truly believe there is a group of owners who won't hire a black man as head coach. . . . Ownership is no dif-

ferent from the makeup of society. Racism is part of that, and we would be lying if we thought that wasn't part of it."[54]

Arguably the most serious problem facing the league is the players' image in the eyes of the fans. Physical contact on the field is an important part of the game, but in recent times, players have carried this same mind-set into their private lives. Cases of college and professional players being arrested on various types of assault charges have become more frequent. How this problem is handled may have a serious impact on the sport's public image.

Despite these problems, college and professional football continue to prosper. There is a continuity that helps maintain interest in the game, despite changing conditions. As Detroit Lions vice chairman Bill Ford Jr. explained in a round table discussion for *Sports Illustrated* magazine, "The one constant we have is the game. Everything surrounding it has changed over the years—the economics, the way we market it—but the game is the same one that my grandfather and my father watched. The game still appeals to people today just as it did 50 years ago."[55] As the twenty-first century begins, the game gives every indication of maintaining that appeal.

Awards and Statistics

Heisman Trophy Winners

Year	Winner	College
1999	Ron Dayne	Wisconsin
1998	Ricky Williams	Texas
1997	Charles Woodson	Michigan
1996	Danny Wuerffel	Florida
1995	Eddie George	Ohio State
1994	Rashaan Salaam	Colorado
1993	Charlie Ward	Florida State
1992	Gino Torretta	Miami
1991	Desmond Howard	Michigan
1990	Ty Detmer	Brigham Young
1989	Andre Ware	Houston
1988	Barry Sanders	Oklahoma State
1987	Tim Brown	Notre Dame
1986	Vinny Testaverde	Miami
1985	Bo Jackson	Auburn
1984	Doug Flutie	Boston College
1983	Mike Rozier	Nebraska
1982	Herschel Walker	Georgia
1981	Marcus Allen	Southern California
1980	George Rogers	South Carolina
1979	Charles White	Southern California
1978	Billy Sims	Oklahoma
1977	Earl Campbell	Texas
1976	Tony Dorsett	Pittsburgh
1975	Archie Griffin	Ohio State
1974	Archie Griffin	Ohio State
1973	John Cappelletti	Penn State
1972	Johnny Rodgers	Nebraska
1971	Pat Sullivan	Auburn
1970	Jim Plunkett	Stanford
1969	Steve Owens	Oklahoma
1968	O.J. Simpson	Southern California

Year	Winner	College
1967	Gary Beban	UCLA
1966	Steve Spurrier	Florida
1965	Mike Garrett	Southern California
1964	John Huarte	Notre Dame
1963	Roger Staubach	Navy
1962	Terry Baker	Oregon State
1961	Ernie Davis	Syracuse
1960	Joe Bellino	Navy
1959	Billy Cannon	LSU
1958	Peter Dawkins	Army
1957	John Crow	Texas A&M
1956	Paul Hornung	Notre Dame
1955	Howard Cassady	Ohio State
1954	Alan Ameche	Wisconsin
1953	John Lattner	Notre Dame
1952	Billy Vessels	Oklahoma
1951	Dick Kazmaier	Princeton
1950	Vic Janowicz	Ohio State
1949	Leon Hart	Notre Dame
1948	Doak Walker	Southern Methodist
1947	John Lujack	Notre Dame
1946	Glenn Davis	Army
1945	Felix Blanchard	Army
1944	Les Horvath	Ohio State
1943	Angelo Bertelli	Notre Dame
1942	Frank Sinkwich	Georgia
1941	Bruce Smith	Minnesota
1940	Tom Harmon	Michigan
1939	Nile Kinnick	Iowa
1938	Davey O'Brien	TCU
1937	Clint Frank	Yale
1936	Larry Kelly	Yale
1935	Jay Berwanger	Chicago

Super Bowl Summaries

Super Bowl	Date	Winner, Conference Loser, Conference	Score	Head Coach	Site
XXXIV	1/30/00	St. Louis, NFC Tennessee, AFC	23 16	Dick Vermeil Jeff Fisher	Atlanta, GA
XXXIII	1/31/99	Denver, AFC Atlanta, NFC	34 19	Mike Shanahan Dan Reeves	Miami, FL
XXXII	1/25/98	Denver, AFC Green Bay, NFC	31 24	Mike Shanahan Mike Holmgren	San Diego, CA
XXXI	1/26/97	Green Bay, NFC New England, AFC	35 21	Mike Holmgren Bill Parcells	New Orleans, LA
XXX	1/28/96	Dallas Cowboys, NFC Pittsburgh, AFC	27 17	Barry Switzer Bill Cowher	Tempe, AZ
XXIX	1/29/95	San Francisco, NFC San Diego, AFC	49 26	George Seifert Bobby Ross	Miami, FL
XXVIII	1/30/94	Dallas, NFC Buffalo, AFC	30 13	Jimmy Johnson Marv Levy	Atlanta, GA
XXVII	1/31/93	Dallas, NFC Buffalo, AFC	52 17	Jimmy Johnson Marv Levy	Pasadena, CA
XXVI	1/26/92	Washington, NFC Buffalo, AFC	37 24	Joe Gibbs Marv Levy	Minneapolis, MN
XXV	1/27/91	N.Y. Giants, NFC Buffalo, AFC	20 19	Bill Parcells Marv Levy	Tampa, FL
XXIV	1/28/90	San Francisco, NFC Denver, AFC	55 10	George Seifert Dan Reeves	New Orleans, LA
XXIII	1/22/89	San Francisco, NFC Cincinnati, AFC	20 16	Bill Walsh Sam Wyche	Miami, FL
XXII	1/31/88	Washington, NFC Denver, AFC	42 10	Joe Gibbs Dan Reeves	San Diego, CA
XXI	1/25/87	N.Y. Giants, NFC Denver, AFC	39 20	Bill Parcells Dan Reeves	Pasadena, CA
XX	1/26/86	Chicago, NFC New England, AFC	46 10	Mike Ditka Raymond Berry	New Orleans, LA
XIX	1/20/85	San Francisco, NFC Miami, AFC	38 16	Bill Walsh Don Shula	Palo Alto, CA
XVIII	1/22/84	L.A. Raiders, AFC Washington, NFC	38 9	Tom Flores Joe Gibbs	Tampa, FL
XVII	1/30/83	Washington, NFC Miami, AFC	27 17	Joe Gibbs Don Shula	Pasadena, CA
XVI	1/24/82	San Francisco, NFC Cincinnati, AFC	26 21	Bill Walsh Forrest Gregg	Pontiac, MI
XV	1/25/81	Oakland, AFC Philadelphia, NFC	27 10	Tom Flores Dick Vermeil	New Orleans, LA

Super Bowl	Date	Winner, Conference Loser, Conference	Score	Head Coach	Site
XIV	1/20/80	Pittsburg, AFC L.A. Rams, NFC	31 19	Chuck Noll Ray Malavasi	Pasadena, CA
XIII	1/21/79	Pittsburgh, AFC Dallas, NFC	35 31	Chuck Noll Tom Landry	Miami, FL
XII	1/15/78	Dallas, NFC Denver, AFC	27 10	Tom Landry Red Miller	New Orleans, LA
XI	1/9/77	Oakland, AFC Minnesota, NFC	32 14	John Madden Bud Grant	Pasadena, CA
X	1/18/76	Pittsburgh, AFC Dallas, NFC	21 17	Chuck Noll Tom Landry	Miami, FL
IX	1/12/75	Pittsburgh, AFC Minnesota, NFC	16 6	Chuck Noll Bud Grant	New Orleans, LA
VIII	1/13/74	Miami, AFC Minnesota, NFC	24 7	Don Shula Bud Grant	Houston, TX
VII	1/14/73	Miami, AFC Washington, NFC	14 7	Don Shula George Allen	Los Angeles, CA
VI	1/16/72	Dallas, NFC Miami, AFC	24 3	Tom Landry Don Shula	New Orleans, LA
V	1/17/71	Baltimore, AFC Dallas, NFC	16 13	Don McCafferty Tom Landry	Miami, FL
IV	1/11/70	Kansas City, AFL Minnesota, NFL	23 7	Hank Stram Bud Grant	New Orleans, LA
III	1/12/69	New York Jets, AFL Baltimore, NFL	16 7	Weeb Ewbank Don Shula	Miami, FL
II	1/14/68	Green Bay, NFL Oakland, AFL	33 14	Vince Lombardi John Rauch	Miami, FL
I	1/15/67	Green Bay, NFL Kansas City, AFL	35 10	Vince Lombardi Hank Stram	Los Angeles, CA

Super Bowl Most Valuable Players

Super Bowl	Position	Player	Team
XXXIV	QB	Kurt Warner	St. Louis
XXXIII	QB	John Elway	Denver
XXXII	RB	Terrell Davis	Denver
XXXI	KR	Desmond Howard	Green Bay
XXX	CB	Larry Brown	Dallas
XXIX	QB	Steve Young	San Francisco
XXVIII	RB	Emmitt Smith	Dallas
XXVII	QB	Troy Aikman	Dallas
XXVI	QB	Mark Rypien	Washington
XXV	RB	Ottis Anderson	N.Y. Giants
XXIV	QB	Joe Montana	San Francisco
XXIII	WR	Jerry Rice	San Francisco
XXII	QB	Doug Williams	Washington
XXI	QB	Phil Simms	N.Y. Giants
XX	DE	Richard Dent	Chicago
XIX	QB	Joe Montana	San Francisco
XVIII	RB	Marcus Allen	L.A. Raiders
XVII	RB	John Riggins	Washington
XVI	QB	Joe Montana	San Francisco
XV	QB	Jim Plunkett	Oakland
XIV	QB	Terry Bradshaw	Pittsburgh

Super Bowl	Position	Player	Team
XIII	QB	Terry Bradshaw	Pittsburgh
XII	DT	Randy White and	Dallas
	DE	Harvey Martin	Dallas
XI	WR	Fred Biletnikoff	Oakland
X	WR	Lynn Swann	Pittsburgh
IX	RB	Franco Harris	Pittsburgh
VIII	RB	Larry Csonka	Miami
VII	S	Jake Scott	Miami
VI	QB	Roger Staubach	Dallas
V	LB	Chuck Howley	Dallas
IV	QB	Len Dawson	Kansas City
III	QB	Joe Namath	N.Y. Jets
II	QB	Bart Starr	Green Bay
I	QB	Bart Starr	Green Bay

Annual NFL Leaders

Individual leaders in NFL (1932–69), AFL (1960–69) and NFC and AFC (since 1970).

Passing

Since 1932, the NFL has used several formulas to determine passing leadership, from Total Yards alone (1932–37) to the current rating system—adopted in 1973—that takes Completions, Completion Percentage, Yards Gained, TD Passes, Interceptions, Interception Percentage, and other factors into account. The quarterbacks listed below all led the league according to the system in use at the time.

NFL–NFC

Year	Att	Cmp	Yds	TD
1999 Kurt Warner, St. L	499	325	4353	41
1998 Randall Cunningham, Min	425	259	3704	34
1997 Steve Young, SF	356	241	3029	19
1996 Steve Young, SF	316	214	2410	14
1995 Brett Favre, GB	570	359	4413	38
1994 Steve Young, SF	461	324	3969	35
1993 Steve Young, SF	462	314	4023	29
1992 Steve Young, SF	402	268	3465	25
1991 Steve Young, SF	279	180	2517	17
1990 Joe Montana, SF	520	321	3944	26
1989 Don Majkowski, GB	599	353	4318	27
1988 Wade Wilson, Min	332	204	2746	15
1987 Joe Montana, SF	398	266	3054	31

Year	Att	Cmp	Yds	TD
1986 Tommy Kramer, Min	372	208	3000	24
1985 Joe Montana, SF	494	303	3653	27
1984 Joe Montana, SF	432	279	3630	28
1983 Steve Bartkowski, Atl	432	274	3167	22
1982 Joe Theismann, Wash	252	161	2033	13
1981 Joe Montana, SF	488	311	3565	19
1980 Ron Jaworski, Phi	451	257	3529	27
1979 Roger Staubach, Dal	461	267	3586	27
1978 Roger Staubach, Dal	413	231	3190	25
1977 Roger Staubach, Dal	361	210	2620	18
1976 James Harris, LA	158	91	1460	8
1975 Fran Tarkenton, Min	425	273	2994	25
1974 Sonny Jurgenson, Wash	167	107	1185	11
1973 Roger Staubach, Dal	286	179	2428	23
1972 Norm Snead, NY	325	196	2307	17
1971 Roger Staubach, Dal	211	126	1882	15
1970 John Brodie, SF	378	223	2941	24
1969 Sonny Jurgenson, Wash	442	274	3102	22
1968 Earl Morral, Bal	317	182	2909	26
1967 Sonny Jurgenson, Wash	508	288	3747	31
1966 Bart Starr, GB	251	156	2257	14
1965 Rudy Bukich, Chi	312	176	2641	20
1964 Bart Starr, GB	272	163	2144	15
1963 Y.A. Tittle, NY	367	221	3145	36
1962 Bart Star, GB	285	178	2438	12
1961 Milt Plum, Cle	302	177	2416	16
1960 Milt Plum, Cle	250	151	2297	21
1959 Charlie Conerly, NY	194	113	1706	14
1958 Eddie LeBaron, Wash	145	79	1365	11
1957 Tommy O'Connell, Cle	110	63	1229	9
1956 Ed Brown, Chi. Bears	168	96	1667	11
1955 Otto Graham, Cle	185	98	1721	15
1954 Norm Van Brocklin, LA	205	113	1736	14
1953 Otto Graham, Cle	258	167	2722	11
1952 Norm Van Brocklin, LA	260	139	2637	13
1951 Bob Waterfield, LA	176	88	1566	13
1950 Norm Van Brocklin, LA	233	127	2061	18
1949 Sammy Baugh, Wash	255	145	1903	18
1948 Tommy Thompson, Phi	246	141	1965	25
1947 Sammy Baugh, Wash	354	210	2938	25
1946 Bob Waterfield, LA	251	127	1747	18
1945 Sammy Baugh, Wash	182	128	1669	11
Sid Luckman, Chi. Bears	217	117	1725	14
1944 Frank Filchock, Wash	147	84	1139	13
1943 Sammy Baugh, Wash	239	133	1754	23
1942 Cecil Isbell, GB	268	146	2021	24

Year	Att	Cmp	Yds	TD
1941 Cecil Isbell, GB	206	117	1479	15
1940 Sammy Baugh, Wash	177	111	1367	12
1939 Parker Hall, Cle. Rams	208	106	1227	9
1938 Ed Danowski, NY	129	70	848	7
1937 Sammy Baugh, Wash	171	81	1127	8
1936 Arnie Herber, GB	173	77	1239	11
1935 Ed Danoski, NY	113	57	794	10
1934 Arnie Herber, GB	115	42	799	8
1933 Harry Newman. NY	136	53	973	11
1932 Arnie Herber, GB	101	37	639	9

Year	Att	Cmp	Yds	TD
1968 Len Dawson, KC	224	131	2109	17
1967 Daryle Lamonica, Oak	425	220	3228	30
1966 Len Dawson, KC	284	159	2527	26
1965 John Hadl, SD	348	174	2798	20
1964 Len Dawson, KC	354	199	2879	30
1963 Tobin Rote, SD	286	170	2510	20
1962 Len Dawson, Dal	310	189	2759	29
1961 George Blanda, Hou	362	187	3330	36
1960 Jack Kemp, LA	406	211	3018	20

AFL–AFC

Year	Att	Cmp	Yds	TD
1999 Peyton Manning, Ind	533	331	4135	26
1998 Vinny Testaverde, NY	421	259	3256	29
1997 Mark Brunell, Jax	435	264	3281	18
1996 John Elway, Den	466	287	3328	26
1995 Jim Harbaugh, Ind	314	200	2575	17
1994 Dan Marino, Mia	615	385	4453	30
1993 John Elway, Den	551	348	4030	25
1992 Warren Moon, Hou	346	224	2521	18
1991 Jim Kelly, Buf	474	304	3844	33
1990 Warren Moon, Hou	584	362	4689	33
1989 Dan Marino, Mia	550	308	3997	24
1988 Boomer Esiason, Cin	388	223	3572	28
1987 Bernie Kosar, Cle	389	241	3033	22
1986 Dan Marino, Mia	623	378	4746	44
1985 Ken O'Brien, NY	488	297	3888	25
1984 Dan Marino, Mia	564	362	5084	48
1983 Dan Marino, Mia	296	173	2210	20
1982 Ken Anderson, Cin	309	218	2495	12
1981 Ken Anderson, Cin	479	300	3753	29
1980 Brian Sipe, Cle	554	337	4132	30
1979 Dan Fouts, SD	530	332	4082	24
1978 Terry Bradshaw, Pit	368	207	2915	28
1977 Bob Griese, Mia	307	180	2252	22
1976 Ken Stabler, Oak	291	194	2737	27
1975 Ken Anderson, Cin	377	228	3169	21
1974 Ken Anderson, Cin	328	213	2667	18
1973 Ken Stabler, Oak	260	163	1997	14
1972 Earl Morrall, Mia	150	83	1360	11
1971 Bob Griese, Mia	263	145	2089	19
1970 Daryle Lamonica, Oak	356	179	2516	22
1969 Greg Cook, Cin	197	106	1854	15

Receptions

NFL–NFC

Year	No	Yds	Avg	TD
1999 Muhsin Muhammad, Car	96	1253	13.1	8
1998 Frank Sanders, Ari	89	1145	12.9	3
1997 Herman Moore, Det	104	1293	12.4	8
1996 Jerry Rice, SF	108	1254	11.6	8
1995 Herman Moore, Det	123	1686	13.7	14
1994 Cris Carter, Min	122	1256	10.3	7
1993 Sterling Sharpe, GB	112	1274	11.4	11
1992 Sterling Sharpe, GB	108	1461	13.5	13
1991 Michael Irvin, Dal	93	1523	16.4	8
1990 Jerry Rice, SF	100	1502	15.0	13
1989 Sterling Sharpe, GB	90	1423	15.8	12
1988 Henry Ellard, LA	86	1414	16.4	10
1987 J.T. Smith, St. L	91	1117	12.3	8
1986 Jerry Rice, SF	86	1570	18.3	15
1985 Roger Craig, SF	92	1016	11.0	6
1984 Art Monk, Wash	106	1372	12.9	7
1983 Roy Green, St. L	78	1227	15.7	14
Charlie Brown, Wash	78	1225	15.7	8
Earnest Gray, NY	78	1139	14.6	5
1982 Dwight Clark, SF	60	913	12.2	5
1981 Dwight Clark, SF	85	1105	13.0	4
1980 Earl Cooper, SF	83	567	6.8	4
1979 Ahmad Rashad, Min	80	1156	14.5	9
1978 Ricky Young, Min	88	704	8.0	5
1977 Ahmad Rashad, Min	51	681	13.4	2
1976 Drew Pearson, Dal	58	806	13.9	6
1975 Chuck Foreman, Min	73	691	9.5	9
1974 Charles Young, Phi	63	696	11.0	3
1973 Harold Carmichael, Phi	67	1116	16.7	9
1972 Harold Jackson, Phi	62	1048	16.9	4
1971 Bob Tucker, NY	59	791	13.4	4

Year	No	Yds	Avg	TD
1970 Dick Gordon, Chi	71	1026	14.5	13
1969 Dan Abramowicz, NO	73	1015	13.9	7
1968 Clifton McNeil, SF	71	994	14.0	7
1967 Charley Taylor, Wash	70	990	14.1	9
1966 Charley Taylor, Wash	72	1119	15.5	12
1965 Dave Parks, SF	80	1344	16.8	12
1964 Johnny Morris, Chi. Bears	93	1200	12.9	10
1963 Bobby Joe Conard, St. L	73	967	13.2	10
1962 Bobby Mitchell, Wash	72	1384	19.2	11
1961 Red Phillips, LA	78	1092	14.0	5
1960 Raymond Berry, Bal	74	1298	17.5	10
1959 Raymond Berry, Bal	66	959	14.5	14
1958 Raymond Berry, Bal	56	794	14.2	9
Pete Retzlaff, Phi	56	766	13.7	2
1957 Billy Wilson, SF	52	757	14.6	6
1956 Billy Wilson, SF	60	889	14.8	5
1955 Pete Pihos, Phi	62	864	13.9	7
1954 Pete Pihos, Phi	60	872	14.5	10
Billy Wilson, SF	60	830	13.8	5
1953 Pete Pihos, Phi	63	1049	16.7	10
1952 Mac Speedie, Cle	62	911	14.7	5
1951 Elroy Hirsch, LA	66	1495	22.7	17
1950 Tom Fears, LA	84	1116	13.3	7
1949 Tom Fears, LA	77	1013	13.2	9
1948 Tom Fears, LA	51	698	13.7	4
1947 Jim Keane, Chi. Bears	64	910	14.2	10
1946 Jim Benton, LA	63	981	15.6	6
1945 Don Hutson, GB	47	834	17.7	9
1944 Don Hutson, GB	58	866	14.9	9
1943 Don Hutson, GB	47	776	16.5	11
1942 Don Hutson, GB	74	1211	16.4	17
1941 Don Hutson, GB	58	739	12.7	10
1940 Don Looney, Phi	58	707	12.2	4
1939 Don Hutson, GB	34	846	24.9	6
1938 Gatnell Tinsley, Chi. Cards	41	516	12.6	1
1937 Don Hutson, GB	41	552	13.5	7
1936 Don Hutson, GB	34	536	15.8	8
1935 Tod Goodwin, NY	26	432	16.6	4
1934 Joe Carter, Phi	16	238	14.9	4
Red Badgro, NY	16	206	12.9	1
1933 Shipwreck Kelly, Bklyn	22	246	11.2	3
1932 Ray Flaherty, NY	21	350	16.7	3

Year	No	Yds	Avg	TD
1997 Tim Brown, Oak	104	1408	13.5	5
1996 Carl Pickens, Cin	100	1180	11.8	12
1995 Carl Pickens, Cin	99	1234	12.5	17
1994 Ben Coates, NE	96	1174	12.2	7
1993 Reggie Langhorne, Ind	85	1038	12.2	3
1992 Haywood Jeffires, Hou	90	913	10.1	9
1991 Haywood Jeffires, Hou	100	1181	11.8	7
1990 Haywood Jeffires, Hou	74	1048	14.2	8
Drew Hill, Hou	74	1019	13.8	5
1989 Andre Reed, Buf	88	1312	14.9	9
1988 Al Toon, NY	93	1067	11.5	5
1987 Al Toon, NY	68	976	14.4	5
1986 Todd Christensen, LA	95	1153	12.1	8
1985 Lionel James, SD	86	1027	11.9	6
1984 Ozzie Newsome, Cle	89	1001	11.2	5
1983 Todd Christensen, LA	92	1247	13.6	12
1982 Kellen Winslow, SD	54	721	13.4	6
1981 Kellen Winslow, SD	88	1075	12.2	10
1980 Kellen Winslow, SD	89	1290	14.5	9
1979 Joe Washington, Bal	82	750	9.1	3
1978 Steve Largent, Sea	71	1168	16.5	8
1977 Lydell Mitchell, Bal	71	620	8.7	4
1976 MacArthur Lane, KC	66	686	10.4	1
1975 Reggie Rucker, Cle	60	770	12.8	3
Lydell Mitchell, Bal	60	544	9.1	4
1974 Lydell Mitchell, Bal	72	544	7.6	2
1973 Fred Willis, Hou	57	371	6.5	1
1972 Fred Biletnikoff, Oak	58	802	13.8	7
1971 Fred Biletnikoff, Oak	61	929	15.2	9
1970 Marlin Briscoe, Buf	57	1036	18.2	8
1969 Lance Alworth, SD	64	1003	15.7	4
1968 Lance Alworth, SD	68	1312	19.3	10
1967 George Sauer, NY	75	1189	15.9	6
1966 Lance Alworth, SD	73	1383	18.9	13
1965 Lionel Taylor, Den	85	1131	13.3	6
1964 Charley Hennigan, Hou	101	1546	15.3	8
1963 Lionel Taylor, Den	78	1101	14.1	10
1962 Lionel Taylor, Den	77	908	11.8	4
1961 Lionel Taylor, Den	100	1176	11.8	4
1960 Lionel Taylor, Den	92	1235	13.4	12

Rushing

AFL–AFC

Year	No	Yds	Avg	TD
1999 Jimmy Smith, Jax	116	1636	14.1	6
1998 O.J. McDuffie, Mia	90	1050	11.7	7

NFL–NFC

Year	Car	Yds	Avg	TD
1999 Stephen Davis, Was	290	1405	4.8	17
1998 Jamal Anderson, Atl	410	1846	4.5	14

Year	Car	Yds	Avg	TD
1997 Barry Sanders, Det	335	2053	6.1	11
1996 Barry Sanders, Det	307	1553	5.1	11
1995 Emmitt Smith, Dal	377	1773	4.7	25
1994 Barry Sanders, Det	331	1883	5.7	7
1993 Emmitt Smith, Dal	283	1486	5.3	9
1992 Emmitt Smith, Dal	373	1713	4.6	18
1991 Emmitt Smith, Dal	365	1563	4.3	12
1990 Barry Sanders, Det	255	1304	5.1	13
1989 Barry Sanders, Det	280	1470	5.3	14
1988 Herschel Walker, Dal	361	1514	4.2	5
1987 Charles White, LA	324	1374	4.2	11
1986 Eric Dickerson, LA	404	1821	4.5	11
1985 Gerald Riggs, Atl	397	1719	4.3	10
1984 Eric Dickerson, LA	379	2105	5.6	14
1983 Eric Dickerson, LA	390	1808	4.6	18
1982 Tony Dorsett, Dal	177	745	4.2	5
1981 George Rodgers, NO	378	1674	4.4	13
1980 Walter Payton, Chi	317	1460	4.6	6
1979 Walter Payton, Chi	369	1610	4.4	14
1978 Walter Payton, Chi	333	1395	4.2	11
1977 Walter Payton, Chi	339	1852	5.5	14
1976 Walter Payton, Chi	311	1390	4.5	13
1975 Jim Otis, St. L	269	1076	4.0	5
1974 Lawerence McCutcheon, LA	236	1109	4.7	3
1973 John Brockington, GB	265	1144	4.3	3
1972 Larry Brown, Wash	285	1216	4.3	8
1971 John Brockington, GB	216	1105	5.1	4
1970 Larry Brown, Wash	237	1125	4.7	5
1969 Gale Sayers, Chi	236	1032	4.4	8
1968 Leroy Kelly, Cle	248	1239	5.0	16
1967 Leroy Kelly, Cle	235	1205	5.1	11
1966 Gale Sayers, Chi	229	1231	5.4	8
1965 Jim Brown, Cle	289	1544	5.3	17
1964 Jim Brown, Cle	280	1446	5.2	7
1963 Jim Brown, Cle	291	1863	6.4	12
1962 Jim Taylor, GB	272	1474	5.4	19
1961 Jim Brown, Cle	305	1408	4.6	8
1960 Jim Brown, Cle	215	1257	5.8	9
1959 Jim Brown, Cle	290	1329	4.6	14
1958 Jim Brown, Cle	257	1527	5.9	17
1957 Jim Brown, Cle	202	942	4.7	9
1956 Rick Casares, Chi. Bears	234	1126	4.8	12
1955 Alan Ameche, Bal	213	961	4.5	9
1954 Joe Perry, SF	173	1049	6.1	8
1953 Joe Perry, SF	192	1018	5.3	10
1952 Dan Towler, LA	156	894	5.7	10

Year	Car	Yds	Avg	TD
1951 Eddie Price, NY Giants	271	971	3.6	7
1950 Marion Motley, Cle	140	810	5.8	3
1949 Steve Van Buren, Phi	263	1146	4.4	11
1948 Steve Van Buren, Phi	201	945	4.7	10
1947 Steve Van Buren, Phi	217	1008	4.6	13
1946 Bill Dudley, Pit	146	604	4.1	3
1945 Steve Van Buren, Phi	143	832	5.8	15
1944 Bill Paschal, NY	196	737	3.8	9
1943 Bill Paschal, NY	147	572	3.9	10
1942 Bill Dudley, Pit	162	696	4.3	5
1941 Pug Manders, Bklyn	111	486	4.4	5
1940 Whizzer White, Det	146	514	3.5	5
1939 Bill Osmanski, Chi. Bears	121	699	5.8	7
1938 Whizzer White, Pit	152	567	3.7	4
1937 Cliff Battles, Wash	216	874	4.0	5
1936 Tuffy Leemans, NY	206	830	4.0	2
1935 Doug Russell, Chi. Cards	140	499	3.6	0
1934 Beattie Feathers, Chi. Bears	119	1004	8.4	8
1933 Jim Musick, Bos	173	809	4.7	5
1932 Cliff Battles, Bos	148	576	3.9	3

AFL–AFC

Year	Car	Yds	Avg	TD
1999 Edgerinn James, Ind	369	1553	4.2	13
1998 Terrell Davis, Den	392	2008	5.1	21
1997 Terrell Davis, Den	369	1750	4.7	15
1996 Terrell Davis, Den	345	1538	4.5	13
1995 Curtis Martin, NE	368	1487	4.0	14
1994 Chris Warren, Sea	333	1545	4.6	9
1993 Thurman Thomas, Buf	355	1315	3.7	6
1992 Barry Foster, Pit	390	1690	4.3	11
1991 Thurman Thomas, Buf	288	1407	4.9	7
1990 Thurman Thomas, Buf	271	1297	4.8	11
1989 Christian Okoye, KC	370	1480	4.0	12
1988 Eric Dickerson, Ind	388	1659	4.3	14
1987 Eric Dickerson, Ind	223	1011	4.5	5
1986 Curt Warner, Sea	319	1481	4.6	13
1985 Marcus Allen, LA	380	1759	4.6	11
1984 Earnest Jackson, SD	296	1179	4.0	8
1983 Curt Warner, Sea	335	1449	4.3	13
1982 Freeman McNeil, N.Y.	151	786	5.2	6
1981 Earl Campbell, Hou	361	1376	3.8	10
1980 Earl Campbell, Hou	373	1934	5.2	13
1979 Earl Campbell, Hou	368	1697	4.6	19
1978 Earl Campbell, Hou	302	1450	4.8	13
1977 Mark van Eeghen, Oak	324	1273	3.9	7
1976 O.J. Simpson, Buf	290	1503	5.2	8

Year	Car	Yds	Avg	TD
1975 O.J. Simpson, Buf	329	1817	5.5	16
1974 Otis Armstrong, Den	263	1407	5.3	9
1973 O.J. Simpson, Buf	332	2003	6.0	12
1972 O.J. Simpson, Buf	292	1251	4.3	6
1971 Floyd Little, Den	284	1133	4.0	6
1970 Floyd Little, Den	209	901	4.3	3
1969 Dickie Post, SD	182	873	4.8	6
1968 Paul Robinson, Cin	238	1023	4.3	8
1967 Jim Nance, Bos	269	1216	4.5	7
1966 Jim Nance, Bos	299	1458	4.9	11
1965 Paul Lowe, SD	222	1121	5.0	7
1964 Cookie Gilchrist, Buf	230	981	4.3	6
1963 Clem Daniels, Oak	215	1099	5.1	3
1962 Cookie Gilchrist, Buf	214	1096	5.1	13
1961 Billy Cannon, Hou	200	948	4.7	6
1960 Abner Haynes, Dal	157	875	5.6	9

Scoring

NFL–NFC

Year	TD	FG	PAT	Pts
1999 Jeff Wilkins, St. L	0	20	64	124
1998 Gary Anderson, Min	0	35	59	164
1997 Richie Cunningham, Dal	0	34	24	126
1996 John Kasay, Car	0	37	34	145
1995 Emmitt Smith, Dal	25	0	0	150
1994 Emmitt Smith, Dal	22	0	0	132
Fuad Reveiz, Min	0	34	30	132
1993 Jason Hanson, Det	0	34	28	130
1992 Chip Lohmiller, Wash	0	30	30	120
Morten Andersen, NO	0	29	33	120
1991 Chip Lohmiller, Wash	0	31	56	149
1990 Chip Lohmiller, Wash	0	30	41	131
1989 Mike Cofer, SF	0	29	49	136
1988 Mike Cofer, SF	0	27	40	121
1987 Jerry Rice, SF	23	0	0	138
1986 Kevin Butler, Chi	0	28	36	120
1985 Kevin Butler, Chi	0	31	51	144
1984 Ray Wersching, SF	0	25	56	131
1983 Mark Moseley, Wash	0	33	62	161
1982 Wendell Tyler, LA	13	0	0	78
1981 Rafael Septien, Dal	0	27	40	121
Eddie Murray, Det	0	25	46	121
1980 Eddie Murray, Det	0	27	35	116
1979 Mark Moseley, Wash	0	25	39	114
1978 Frank Corral, LA	0	29	31	118
1977 Walter Payton, Chi	16	0	0	96

Year	TD	FG	PAT	Pts
1976 Mark Moseley, Wash	0	22	31	97
1975 Chuck Foreman, Min	22	0	0	132
1974 Chester Marcol, GB	0	25	19	94
1973 David Ray, LA	0	30	40	130
1972 Chester Marcol, GB	0	33	29	128
1971 Curt Knight, Wash	0	29	27	114
1970 Fred Cox, Min	0	30	35	125
1969 Fred Cox, Min	0	26	43	121
1968 Leroy Kelly, Cle	20	0	0	120
1967 Jim Bakken, St. L	0	27	36	117
1966 Bruce Gossett, LA	0	28	29	113
1965 Gale Sayers, Chi	22	0	0	132
1964 Lenny Moore, Bal	20	0	0	120
1963 Don Chandler, NY	0	18	52	106
1962 Jim Taylor, GB	19	0	0	114
1961 Paul Hornung, GB	10	15	41	146
1960 Paul Hornung, GB	15	15	41	176
1959 Paul Hornung, GB	7	7	31	94
1958 Jim Brown, Cle	18	0	0	108
1957 Sam Baker, Wash	1	14	29	77
Lou Groza, Cle	0	15	32	77
1956 Bobby Layne, Det	5	12	33	99
1955 Doak Walker, Det	7	9	27	96
1954 Bobby Walston, Phi	11	4	36	114
1953 Gordy Soltau, SF	6	10	48	114
1952 Gordy Soltau, SF	7	6	34	94
1951 Elroy Hirsch, LA	17	0	0	102
1950 Doak Walker, Det	11	8	38	128
1949 Gene Roberts, NY Giants	17	0	0	102
Pat Harder, Chi. Cards	8	3	45	102
1948 Pat Harder, Chi. Cards	6	7	53	110
1947 Pat Harder, Chi. Cards	7	7	39	102
1946 Ted Fritsch, GB	10	9	13	100
1945 Steve Van Buren, Phi	18	0	2	110
1944 Don Hutson, GB	9	0	31	85
1943 Don Hutson, GB	12	3	26	117
1942 Don Hutson, GB	17	1	33	138
1941 Don Hutson, GB	12	1	20	95
1940 Don Hutson, GB	7	0	15	57
1939 Andy Farkas, Wash	11	0	2	68
1938 Clarke Hinkle, GB	7	3	7	58
1937 Jack Manders, Chi. Bears	5	8	15	69
1936 Dutch Clark, Det.	7	4	19	73
1935 Dutch Clark, Det.	6	1	16	55
1934 Jack Manders, Chi. Bears	3	10	31	79
1933 Glenn Presnell, Portsmouth	6	6	10	64
Ken Strong, NY	6	5	13	64
1932 Dutch Clark, Portsmouth	6	3	10	55

Scoring

AFL–AFC

Year	TD	FG	PAT	Pts
1999 Mike Vanderjagt, Ind	0	34	43	145
1998 Steve Christie, Buf	0	33	41	140
1997 Mike Hollis, Jax	0	31	41	134
1996 Cary Blanchard, Ind	0	36	27	135
1995 Norm Johnson, Pit	0	34	39	141
1994 John Carney, SD	0	34	33	135
1993 Jeff Jaeger, LA	0	35	27	132
1992 Pete Stoyanovich, Mia	0	30	34	124
1991 Pete Stoyanovich, Mia	0	31	28	121
1990 Nick Lowery, KC	0	34	37	139
1989 David Treadwell, Den	0	27	39	120
1988 Scott Norwood, Buf	0	32	33	129
1987 Jim Breech, Cin	0	24	25	97
1986 Tony Franklin, NE	0	32	44	140
1985 Gary Anderson, Pit	0	33	40	139
1984 Gary Anderson, Pit	0	24	45	117
1983 Gary Anderson, Pit	0	27	38	119
1982 Marcus Allen, LA	14	0	0	84

Year	TD	FG	PAT	Pts
1981 Nick Lowery, KC	0	26	37	115
Jim Breech, Cin	0	22	49	115
1980 John Smith, NE	0	26	51	129
1979 John Smith, NE	0	23	46	115
1978 Pat Leahy, NY	0	22	41	107
1977 Errol Mann, Oak	0	20	39	99
1976 Toni Linhart, Bal	0	20	49	109
1975 O.J. Simpson, Buf	23	0	0	138
1974 Roy Gerela, Pit	0	20	33	93
1973 Roy Gerela, Pit	0	29	36	123
1972 Bobby Howfield, NY	0	27	40	121
1971 Garo Yepremian, Mia	0	28	33	117
1970 Jan Stenerud, KC	0	30	26	116
1969 Jim Turner, NY	0	32	33	129
1968 Jim Turner, NY	0	34	43	145
1967 George Blanda, Oak	0	20	56	116
1966 Gino Cappelletti, Bos	6	16	35	119
1965 Gino Cappelletti, Bos	9	17	27	132
1964 Gino Cappelletti, Bos	7	25	36	155
1963 Gino Cappelletti, Bos	2	22	35	113
1962 Gene Mingo, Den	4	27	32	137
1961 Gino Cappelletti, Bos	8	17	48	147
1960 Gene Mingo, Den	6	18	33	123

Notes

Introduction: A Collision Sport

1. Quoted in Bob Carroll et al., eds., *Total Football*. New York: Harper-Collins, 1997, p. 446.
2. Quoted in Carroll et al., *Total Football*, p. 446.
3. Quoted in Dave Anderson, *The Story of Football*. New York: Morrow, 1997, p. 151.
4. Quoted in Carroll et al., *Total Football*, p. 229.
5. Quoted in Joseph Hession, *Forty Niners: Looking Back*. San Francisco: Foghorn Press, 1986, p. 69.

Chapter 1: The Evolution of Rugby Football

6. Tom Bennett et al., eds., *The NFL's Official Encyclopedic History of Professional Football*. New York: MacMillan, 1977, p. 10.
7. Quoted in Lee Green, *Sportswit.* New York: Fawcett Crest, 1984, p. 72.
8. Quoted in Bennett et al., *The NFL's Official Encyclopedic History of Professional Football*, p. 11.
9. Quoted in Bennett et al., *The NFL's Official Encyclopedic History of Professional Football*, p. 10.

Chapter 2: Playing the Game

10. Quoted in Peter King, *Football: A History of the Professional Game*. New York: Time, 1996, pp. 17–18.
11. Quoted in Anderson, *The Story of Football*, p. 14.
12. Quoted in Riley Ondek, "Birth of the Bomb," *Sports History*, March 1988, p. 37.
13. Quoted in Green, *Sportswit*, p. 179.
14. Quoted in Ondek, "Birth of the Bomb," p. 39.
15. Gene Brown, ed., *The New York Times Encyclopedia of Sports—Football*. New York: Arno Press, 1979, p. 7.

Chapter 3: The Pros Take the Field

16. Quoted in Robert W. Peterson, *Pigskin: The Early Years of Pro Football*. New York: Oxford University Press, 1997, p. 86.
17. Quoted in Bennett et al., *The NFL's Official Encyclopedic History of Professional Football*, p. 11.
18. Peterson, *Pigskin*, p. 29.
19. Peterson, *Pigskin*, p. 31.
20. Quoted in Rick Korch, "Pro Football's Bear Beginnings," *Sports History*, January 1988, p. 26.
21. Quoted in Anderson, *The Story of Football*, p. 31.
22. Peterson, *Pigskin*, p. 69.
23. Quoted in Peterson, *Pigskin*, p. 78.
24. Peterson, *Pigskin*, p. 87.

25. John Underwood, "Was He the Greatest of All Time?" *Sports Illustrated*, September 4, 1985, p. 118.
26. Quoted in Peterson, *Pigskin*, p. 120.

Chapter 4: A National Obsession

27. Quoted in Peterson, *Pigskin*, p. 138.
28. Quoted in Peterson, *Pigskin*, p. 134.
29. Quoted in Carroll et al., *Total Football*, p. 23.
30. Quoted in Peterson, *Pigskin*, p. 148.
31. Quoted in Peterson, *Pigskin*, p. 192
32. Quoted in Hank Hersch, *Greatest Football Games of All Time*. New York: Time, 1997, p. 29.
33. Quoted in Carroll et al., *Total Football*, pp. 445–446.
34. Quoted in Anderson, *The Story of Football*, p. 55.
35. Quoted in Carroll et al., *Total Football*, p. 102.
36. Quoted in King, *Football*, p. 49.

Chapter 5: The Greats of the Game

37. Quoted in Carroll et al., *Total Football*, p. 265.
38. Quoted in Peter King, "Letting Go," *Sports Illustrated*, March 20, 2000, p. 65.
39. Quoted in King, *Football*, p. 116.
40. Quoted in Anderson, *The Story of Football*, pp. 37–38.
41. Quoted in Carroll et al., *Total Football*, p. 223.
42. Quoted in King, *Football*, p. 108.
43. Quoted in King, *Football*, p. 108.
44. Quoted in Ronald L. Mendell and Timothy B. Phares, *Who's Who in Football*. New Rochelle, NY: Arlington House, 1974, p. 124.
45. Quoted in Paul Zimmerman, "The Bronk and the Gazelle," *Sports Illustrated*, September 11, 1989, p. 134.
46. Quoted in John Garrity, "The Game's Greatest Receiver," *Sports Illustrated* (special issue), Fall 1995, p. 46.
47. Quoted in Carroll et al., *Total Football*, p. 240.
48. Quoted in King, *Football*, p. 114.
49. Quoted in Carroll et al., *Total Football*, p. 225.
50. Quoted in Anderson, *The Story of Football*, p. 133.
51. Quoted in Anderson, *The Story of Football*, p. 134.
52. Quoted in Jeffrey Shelman, "Only one question: Was he the greatest?" *Cincinnati Post*, 1998. www.cincypost.com/sports/1998/best080198.html.
53. Quoted in King, *Football*, p. 198.

Epilogue: Entering the Twenty-First Century

54. Quoted in Peter King, "Game Plan," *Sports Illustrated*, August 30, 1999, p. 115.
55. Quoted in King, "Game Plan," p. 108.

For Further Reading

Books

Bob Carroll, *100 Greatest Running Backs*. New York: Crescent Books, 1989. Looks at the workhorses who grind out the yards and put points on the board.

Tim Cohane, *Great College Football Coaches of the Twenties and Thirties*. New Rochelle, NY: Arlington House, 1973. Detailed biographies of many of the greatest college coaches in the early days of the game.

Tim Crothers, *Greatest Teams: The Most Dominant Powerhouses in Sports*. New York: Time, 1998. This volume in the lavishly illustrated series of *Sports Illustrated* books looks at the greatest sports teams of all time.

George Halas, with Gwen Morgan and Arthur Veysey, *Halas by Halas*. New York: McGraw-Hill, 1979. The story of George Halas, the "Father of the NFL."

Austin Murphy, *The Super Bowl: Sport's Greatest Championship*. New York: Time, 1998. This *Sports Illustrated* series volume examines football's ultimate showcase, with many full-color photographs.

Davis S. Neft and Richard Cohen, *The Sports Encyclopedia: Pro Football*. New York: St. Martin's Press, 1987. Definitive statistical history of professional football in the modern era, from 1960 to 1986.

Bert Randolph Sugar, ed., *The SEC*. Indianapolis: Bobbs-Merrill Company, 1979. Detailed, pictorial history of football in the Southeastern Conference.

Richard Whittingham, *The Fireside Book of Pro Football*. New York: Simon & Schuster, 1989. Collection of writings on professional football.

Websites

College Football Hall of Fame (www.collegefootball.org). The official website of college football's shrine to its immortals.

NCAA Football (www.ncaafootball.net). Football as seen through the eyes of the National Collegiate Athletic Association.

National Football League (www.nfl.com). The official website of pro football's oldest established league.

Pro Football Hall of Fame (www.profootballhof.com). The official website of the shrine to the men who made pro football what it is today.

Super Bowl (www.SuperBowl.com). NFL website that covers the history of pro football's championship games.

Works Consulted

Books

Dave Anderson, *The Story of Football*. New York: Morrow, 1997. Pulitzer Prize–winning sportswriter updates his 1985 version of the history of the game.

Tom Bennett, et al., eds., *The NFL's Official Encyclopedic History of Professional Football*. New York: Macmillan, 1977. One of the most authoritative and complete accounts of the players, records, and events in the first six decades of the National Football League.

Gene Brown, ed., *The New York Times Encyclopedia of Sports—Football*. New York: Arno Press, 1979. A collection of articles from the *New York Times* tracing the history of football from 1905 to 1979.

Bob Carroll et al., eds., *Total Football*. New York: HarperCollins, 1997. Comprehensive football reference containing statistics and historical essays.

Lee Green, *Sportswit*. New York: Fawcett Crest, 1984. Collection of sports quotes on a variety of subjects.

Hank Hersch, *Greatest Football Games of All Time*. New York: Time, 1997. *Sports Illustrated* series volume that examines pro football's all-time classic games.

Joseph Hession, *Forty Niners: Looking Back*. San Francisco: Foghorn Press, 1986. Hession gives the complete story of the San Francisco 49ers from their 1946 beginnings through the 1984 season.

Ford Hovis, ed., *The Sports Encyclopedia*. New York: Praeger Publishers, 1976. Contains descriptions of modern-day sports, with sections on history, equipment, strategy, and scoring.

Peter King, *Football: A History of the Professional Game*. New York: Time, 1996. *Sports Illustrated* series volume that is an authoritative tribute to America's most popular sport.

Ronald L. Mendell and Timothy B. Phares, *Who's Who in Football*. New Rochelle, NY: Arlington House, 1974. Profiles more than 1,400 football personalities from the game's birth through 1973.

Robert W. Peterson, *Pigskin: The Early Years of Pro Football*. New York: Oxford University Press, 1997. Detailed examination of the early years of the game, up through the 1958 NFL Championship game.

Mark Stewart, *Football: A History of the Gridiron Game*. New York: Franklin Watts, 1998. Discusses the origins and evolution of the sport, as well as important events and personalities in its history.

Periodicals

Bob Carroll and Bob Barnett, "Black Hats in a Golden Age," *Sports Heritage*, January/February 1987.

John Garrity, "The Game's Greatest Receiver," *Sports Illustrated* (special issue), Fall 1995.

Peter King, "Game Plan," *Sports Illustrated*, August 30, 1999.

Peter King, "Letting Go," *Sports Illustrated*, March 20, 2000.

Rick Korch, "Pro Football's Bear Beginnings," *Sports History*, January 1988.

Riley Ondek, "Birth of the Bomb," *Sports History*, March 1988.

John Underwood, "Was He the Greatest of All Time?" *Sports Illustrated*, September 4, 1985.

Jeffry D. Wert, "Days of Iron Men," *Sports History*, November 1987.

Jeffry D. Wert, "Protection Against Organized Mayhem," *Sports History*, January 1988.

Paul Zimmerman, "The Bronk and the Gazelle," *Sports Illustrated*, September 11, 1989.

Internet Sources

Jeffrey Shelman, "Only one question: Was he the greatest?" *Cincinnati Post,* 1998. www.cincypost.com/sports/1998/best080 198.html

Natalie McRae, "The Historic Game of Calcio in Costume," 1998. www.firenze.net /events/culture/calcio.html

Websites

Arena Football (www.arenafootball.com) The official website of the Arena Football League includes information on star players, league history, and team records.

Index

Picture Credits

About the Author

John F. Grabowski is a native of Brooklyn, New York. He holds a bachelor's degree in psychology from City College of New York and a master's degree in educational psychology from Teacher's College, Columbia University. He has been a teacher for thirty-one years, as well as a freelance writer, specializing in the fields of sports, education, and comedy. His body of published work includes twenty-two books; a nationally syndicated sports column; consultation on several math textbooks; articles for newspapers, magazines, and the programs of professional sports teams; and comedy material sold to Jay Leno, Joan Rivers, and numerous other comics. He and his wife, Patricia, live in Staten Island with their daughter, Elizabeth.